Ancient
ROMAN
Holidays

Ancient
ROMAN
Holidays

Mab Borden

The Witches' Almanac
Providence, Rhode Island

Address all inquiries and information to
THE WITCHES' ALMANAC, LTD.
P.O. Box 25239
Providence, RI 02905-7700

Softcover:
13-ISBN: 978-1-938918-96-4
eBook
978-1-881098-97-3

First Printing February 2024

Printed in USA

1 2 3 4 5 6 7 8 9 10

Caesaris arma canant alii: nos Caesaris aras
et quoscumque sacris addidit ille dies.

Let others sing of Caesar's wars—we sing of Caesar's
altars and of whatever days he added to the sacred rites.

–Ovid, *Fasti*,
tr. Mab Borden

Table of Contents

Introduction

Roman culture is first and foremost urban, especially compared to the rest of the ancient world. While Thebes was the largest city in the world under the eighteenth dynasty with 80,000 people and around 150,000 people lived in Athens at its peak, a million people lived in the city of Rome by the end of the pagan era. A great deal of what is distinctly Roman can be readily understood if you keep in mind how very crowded it was. For example, the lovely stone temples and stoas of the Greeks and the Etruscans received a nod from Roman architects in the overall aesthetic of Roman buildings, but everything was translated into concrete. Marble is simply not strong enough to span the distances required to shelter the masses, while concrete is cheap, strong and versatile. And while the Greeks envisioned a realm of the Gods with twelve primary inhabitants and saw their dead as shades drifting through the fields of the Underworld, Ovid imagined the Roman worlds of both the dead and the heavens as cities teeming with people.

Just as human cities can seem chaotic, so can Roman cosmology. The Roman spiritual world is crowded and the Gods of the Romans varied beyond what many modern people might think of as Gods. There were Olympian Gods, Sabine, Latin and Etruscan Gods, other imported Gods and land spirits who protected rivers, springs and wells. There were ancestors, ancestors who became Gods and semi-ancestral household Gods who brought fortune to the family. There were deified concepts such as luck, peace and right-mindedness who were not simply ideas, but who received sacrifice at their altars just as more personalized deities did, and who were frequently depicted in human form. There were collectives of Gods organized by function or cosmological region, such as Gods of childbirth or Gods of Earth, and their numbers were not always clear.

Maintaining all of these Gods with all of their temples and feast days was an obligation of the state. Roman religion was propitiatory and the maintenance of religion and the maintenance of a field required a similar mindset. Consider the Latin word *cultus*, a multi-faceted word meaning cultivated, inhabited, tilled, honored, worshipped, tended and adorned. While at first glance the Roman calendar seems awfully packed with sacrifices and festivals, remember that farmers who expect a good yield care for their fields daily—all their fields, not just the garden patch behind the house. Similarly, Rome cared for her Gods regularly, including those deities whose origins are vague and those festivals so old that the reasons for them had fallen out of memory long before they had a chance to be written about.

Roman religion was driven primarily by fear of various powers—who were easily offended—and rituals focused on keeping them from doing harm to mortals. If someone did offend the dead or the Gods, rituals of expiation purified people from involuntary offenses such as mistakes made in rituals. They could also purify unknown offenses that were made clear through signs of the anger of the Gods, such as lightning or other ill omens. The Romans also propitiated hostile spirits before they could cause harm to the individual, family or state.

Rome considered herself pious, indicating a broad set of obligations within society as well as within religion. Piety did not imply religious belief—Roman religion is characterized by ritual nearly devoid of theology. Many Romans were careful to attend to their religious duties without necessarily believing in the Gods. For example, the writer Horace, who wrote numerous hymns to Gods—many featured in this book—typically did so symbolically, politically or playfully. Some of the translations included here are edited to remove the lines that seem to the modern reader to be random insertions of praise to politicians and women in the midst of an otherwise coherent prayer, but these lines were—for Horace—the driving purpose of the poems and the religious references served to support them, not the other way around. He was nonetheless pious because he scrupulously attended to religious ritual. Roman *pietas* is a widely applicable value of loyalty, duty, right relationship and keeping with tradition that circumscribed interactions between living people, between people and their ancestors, between social classes, between people and the Gods, between people and the state and between the state and the Gods. Maintaining piety was an essential obligation of the state—the military and economic success of Rome depended on the goodwill of the Gods! While a sacrifice to the personified idea of luck or to the deity of an imported cult or to the spirit of a river might not seem like the state's highest concern to the modern person on first glance, maintaining right relationship with the divine—all of them—was an urgent and vital matter. This is not to say that all Gods were equally important in Rome. That was very much not the case! Some cults were far more central and essential than others—for example, the cult of Vesta and those of the Capitoline triad of Jupiter, Juno and Minerva.

Many of the festivals described in this book are anniversaries of the dedications of temples. Some temples also celebrated the anniversaries of the days on which they were rededicated after renovation. These were important dates for venerating the Gods of those temples as in ancient times, there would be special sacrifices on the *dies natalis* (birthday) of a temple each year. Like honoring the feast-day of a saint, these were important days to remember to connect with many of the less well-known Gods of Rome. Failing to celebrate the Gods' *feriae* (festivals) meant risking their wrath. Maintaining the traditional rites and customs, though, ensured their benevolence.

THE ROMAN CALENDAR

Days of the month in Rome were counted in numbers from or to certain fixed days: the *Kalends*, the *Nones* and the *Ides*. These probably began as sightings of the various phases of the Moon, but by the historical period, they were simply specific days and the calendar was primarily solar. The Kalends of the month was the first day and was always sacred to Juno, the nones was either the fifth or the seventh, and the ides was either the thirteenth or the fifteenth, all depending on whether the month was full (with thirty-one days) or hollow (with thirty days.) These fixed days are marked in the overview in each chapter. Additionally, days could be considered lucky and unlucky in different degrees. While some were generally unlucky, on most festival days, courts would be closed and it wasn't acceptable to begin business ventures—but that was less about luck and more about propriety.

The Roman calendar itself changed significantly over time. It originally consisted of ten months, beginning in March. Most of their names are familiar: *Martius* (the month of Mars,) *Aprilis* (the month of Aphrodite,) *Maius* (the month of Maia,) *Junius* (the month of Juno,) *Quintilis* (the fifth month,) *Sextilis* (the sixth month,) *September, October, November* and *December*. The March start date was likely influenced by calendars from the Near East that aligned starting points with the astrological new year—when the Sun leaves the constellation of Pisces and moves into Aries at the Spring Equinox. Because the ideal Roman was the farmer-soldier-statesman, though, it was a very natural fit for the year to begin with the new agricultural and military ventures in the Spring.

This ten-month calendar was composed of thirty-eight market weeks: eight-day periods called *nundinae*. After the market weeks had run out, there was a gap for Winter of an imprecise number of days that lasted roughly two modern months. This was later divided into two months, which were added to the calendar in the period of the Roman Republic under the names *Januarius* (the month of Janus) and *Februarius* (the month of purification.) In the second century BCE, the beginning of the year was shifted to January. The month names remained the same, however, so that the modern month of July, for example, was still called *Quintilis* (the fifth month) even after it had become the seventh month on the new calendar. This traditional naming persists in modern times—the Roman Republican calendrical reform is the reason that the modern months of September, October, November and December are the ninth, tenth, eleventh and twelfth months, even though their names mean seventh, eighth, ninth and tenth, respectively.

Even after these reforms, though, this system did not add up to a complete solar cycle and the calendar drifted significantly over time, requiring additional reforms. In 46 BCE Julius Caesar added ten days to the calendar and leap days every three years (an error which was later adjusted to every four years.) Shortly after Caesar's death, Mark Antony changed the name of Quintilis to Julius, to honor Julius Caesar's birthday. In 8 BCE, the Roman populace voted to rename Sextilis to Augustus in honor of their ruler Augustus, who brought peace from the civil wars that had been scourging Rome for nearly a century. The Julian calendar was again slightly adjusted by Pope Gregory XIII in the 16th century, resulting in the calendar most widely used in modern times.

Because the audience of this book is the modern reader rather than the ancient, the month names and order presented here follow the Roman calendar after the Julian reforms and the name changes of the 1st century BCE. This is the basis of the modern calendar and the simplest to convert for most purposes.

PRIESTHOODS AND RELIGIOUS PRACTICES

The more significant state cults were tended by *flamens* (priests.) Jupiter, Quirinus (the deified form of Romulus, the founder of Rome,) and Mars had major flamens. These were called the flamen Dialis, the flamen Quirinalis and the flamen Martialis. The pontifical college—the governmental body of the priesthood—was made up of these three as well as twelve other minor flamens. Each of the major priesthoods was appointed for life and came with significant restrictions as well as privileges. Women held fewer priestly roles but some came with great influence. The wife of the flamen Dialis served as a priestess of Juno, and the head of the Vestals had a seat on the pontifical college.

In addition to presiding over festivals, the flamens offered sacrifices on a daily basis. In contrast, the *pontifices* (which also means "priests") were members of another priestly college, which concerned themselves with sacred matters more broadly, including sacrifices and rites conducted by individuals as well as those managed by the state. There were also augurs who read omens and haruspices who interpreted the signs in the entrails of sacrificed animals.

The basis of Roman religion was sacrifice. This could be blood offerings of domestic animals or bloodless offerings such as wine, cakes, garlands, incense and grain. Many sacrifices included both, with bloodless offerings preceding the slaughter of the animals. For the modern Pagan, there is no need to revive the bloody business of ritual slaughter unless you already lead a lifestyle in which you kill your own dinner. Garlands and incense accompanied by offering cakes are perfectly traditional. Ovid said that juniper was offered before exotic resins were available, and there are even ancient recipes for offering cakes which can be easily replicated today.

In all cases, the altar was approached with covered head and washed hands, in a spirit of piety. Priests did not slaughter animals themselves— the victims were both handled and killed by slaves. These same slaves led the animals in the procession to the altar. Generally, altars were outside temples and a person making an offering could invite friends and family to attend. After hands were washed, a priest would call for silence before the main officiant covered his head and began making the offerings. These were accompanied by prayers which were formulaic and had to be recited precisely and perfectly, or the rite would have to be redone.

Because of this emphasis on meticulous execution, if you find that you want to begin a regular practice of venerating Roman Gods beyond simply incorporating some of the holidays and practices described in this book into your current worship, you would do well to seek out reconstructionist groups for guidance. The purpose of this book is to describe the ancient rituals and holidays for modern Pagans as faithfully as possible to the ancient sources, not to adapt them to modern settings—that is the business of the individual ritualist or working group. Moreover, much of ancient religion happened within the home, and this book deals almost exclusively with state festivals. Roman religion is complex and—as with all reconstructions—some aspects are more logistically feasible than others to recreate and there is a huge amount of research involved in truly embracing an ancient tradition. There are organizations and individuals who have already done a great deal of that work and who could guide you in more detail for setting up a regular practice.

THE NATURE OF ROME AND THE NATURE OF THE GODS

Rome fits poorly into romantic fantasies of historical Paganism, which tend to glorify the simple and bucolic aspects of preindustrial, rural life. Indeed, Rome is no idealized rustic village but a vast city whose citizens had access to running water, welfare and a fire department. It can be equally characterized by its street gangs, corrupt politicians and gerrymandering-like election systems that ensured that power stayed in the hands of those who were already powerful. While the wealthy had more traditional houses, most of the population lived in multi-story high rises and anyone who's had a slumlord can relate to the tenants of Crassus, who said that he was glad one of the apartment buildings he owned was so poorly built that it had collapsed—he could charge higher rents for a new building. Many readers may find the Rome described in this book to be at once surprisingly familiar and also jarringly different from modern societies. Some of these differences may be distasteful and others outright abhorrent. Roman society had a high degree of violence, both casual and institutional. Social classes were extremely rigid and the upper-class patricians and lower-class plebeians had different legal and political rights, which extended to what clothing they were permitted to wear. Slavery was widespread and required no dehumanization of the enslaved to be morally justifiable—it was simply acceptable to own another human being and both possible and desirable to own one more skilled or better educated than yourself. Many Roman slaves were war captives, and others had been Roman infants who had been left out to die because they were illegitimate or otherwise unwanted and had been picked up by slave traders and later sold. This was common and acceptable. Roman Paganism had little to say about ethical considerations because it was not a moral force. While a few myths do depict the Gods testing certain aspects of piety such as the obligations of hospitality, the divine was generally disinterested in the goodness of humankind. You gained the favor of the Gods by tending to their cults, not by being good, whether by ancient or modern standards. Guidelines for moral living were the concern of tradition and philosophy, not religion. The philosophies of both Greece and Rome—of Plato, Aristotle, Zeno and others—were seen by their adherents alternately as competitors to traditional polytheistic religion or as necessary addendums to it, because philosophy furnished humankind with moral guidelines that simply weren't within the purview of Roman Paganism. After all, why would the spirit of a well care if you'd cheated at dice?

While land and water spirits might seem disconnected from human affairs, the greater Gods were very much intertwined with the life of the city. But while they might impose certain restrictions on their priesthood—for example the required chastity of the Vestals—they were not generally inclined to concern themselves with the ethical intricacies of human choices. They may have looked human and acted it in some stories, but they were embodiments of *numen*, a divine force or power, a spirit or divinity that inspires awe. Seneca describes it as something you might sense in a secluded spot in nature, an idea most readers will readily understand. The Gods are simply powers.

✳

If ever you have happened upon a grove crowded with ancient trees far taller than their usual height, their intertwining branches forming a cloak that blocks the view of the sky, then the height of the forest and the solitude of the place and your wonder at such dense, unbroken shade in the open space will make you believe that a divine power is present. Or if some grotto carved out by the deep wearing away of the stone holds up a mountain, a place not made by hands but hollowed out to such openness by natural causes, your spirit will be struck by some instinctive feeling of sanctity. We pray at the sources of great rivers, we keep altars where vast streams suddenly rush out from hidden places, we venerate hot springs, and we consecrate certain lakes either because of their darkness or their immeasurable depth.

–Seneca the Younger
tr. Mab Borden

Temple of Neptune

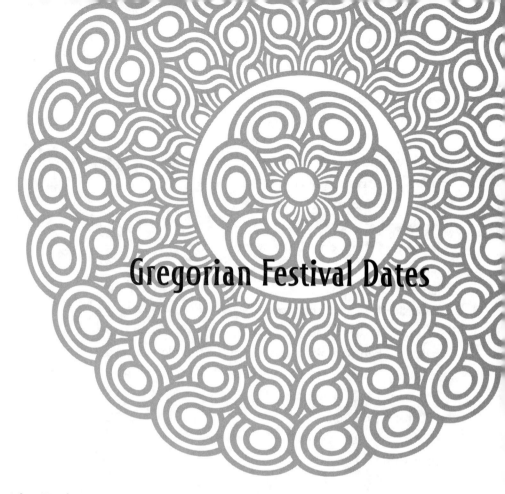

Gregorian Festival Dates

The earliest publicly agreed-upon dates in Rome probably came from observations of the Moon. The three markers in the month in historical times—the Kalends, the Nones and the Ides—probably began at some early point with someone watching the sky at night and declaring sightings of the New Moon, the first quarter Moon and the Full Moon. All other dates were counts referring to these originally observable markers. There was no 11th or 30th—of the month—there was three days before the Ides and two days before the Kalends (the Romans counted inclusively.) Therefore, to the Romans, the Fishermen's Games are three days after the Nones of June and the feast of Fontinalia falls three days before the Ides of October, whereas to the modern reader, these dates are June 7th and October 13th.

January 1: dies natalis of the temple of Aesculapius
January 1: dies natalis of the temple of Vediovis
January 3: Compitalia (moveable)
January 5: dies natalis of the shrine of Vica Pota
January 9: Agonalia of Janus
January 11: Juturnalia
January 11 and 15: Carmentalia
January 24–26: Feriae Sementivae
January 27: Ludi Castores
January 27: dies natalis of the temple of Castor and Pollux
February 1: sacra at the grove of Alernus
February 1: dies natalis of the temple of Juno Sospita
February February 5: dies natalis of the temple of Concordia
February 13: Festival of Faunus
February 13–21: Parentalia
February 15: Lupercalia
February 17: Quirinalia, the Feast of the Fools
February 21: Feralia
February 22: Caristia
February 23: Terminalia
February 24: Regifugium
Moveable feast in February: Amburbium
February 27: Equirria
Moveable feast before the 17 of February: Fornacalia
March 1: Feriae Marti and dies natalis of Mars
March 1: Matronalia
March 7: dies natalis of the Temple of Vediovis (Capitoline)
March 14: Equirria
March 15: Festival of Anna Perenna
March 15: Feriae Iovi
March 16–17: procession of the Argei

March 17: Agonalia of Mars

March 17: Liberalia

March 19: Quinquatria

March 23: Tubilustrium

March 31: dies natalis of the Temple of Luna

April 1: Veneralia

April 1: rites of Fortuna Virilis

April 4–10: Ludi Megalenses

April 5: dies natalis of the temple of Fortuna Publica

April 12–19: Cerealia

April 13: dies natalis of the Temple of Jupiter Victor

April 15: Fordicidia

April 21: dies natalis of Rome

April 21: Parilia

April 23: Vinalia

April 25: Robigalia

April 27: Floralia

Moveable feast in April: Feriae Latinae

May 1: day of the Lares Praestites

May 1: dies natalis of the temple of Bona Dea

May 3: celebration for Flora

May 9, 11 and 13: Lemuria

May 14: procession of the Argei

May 14: dies natalis of the temple of Mars Invictus

May 15: Feriae of Jove

May 15: Mercuralia

May 21: Agonalia

May 21: festival of Vediovis

May 23: Feriae of Vulcan

May 23: Tubilustrium

May 25: dies natalis of the temple of Fortuna Primigenia

Moveable feast in May: Ambarvalia

June 1: festival of Cardea

June 1: dies natalis of the temple of Juno Moneta

June 1: dies natalis of the temple of Mars

June 1: dies natalis of the temple of the Tempestates

June 3: dies natalis of the temple of Bellona

June 4: dies natalis of the temple of Hercules Custos

June 5: dies natalis of the temple of Dius Fidius

June 7: Ludi Piscatorii, the Fishermen's Games

June 7–15: Vestalia

June 8: dies natalis of the temple of Mens Bona

June 11: Matralia for Mater Matuta

June 11: dies natalis of the temple of Fortuna in the Forum Boarium

June 13–15: Quinquatrus Minisculae

June 19: dies natalis of the temple of Minerva on the Aventine

June 20: anniversary of the temple of Summanus

June 24: Festival of Fors Fortuna

June 27: honoring the Lares

June 27: dies natalis of the temple of Jupiter Stator

June 29: dies natalis of the temple of Hercules Musarum

Moveable feast in June: Taurian Games, usually held around the 25–26

July 1: dies natalis of the temple of Juno Felicitas

July 5: Poplifugia

July 6: dies natalis of the temple of Fortuna Muliebris

July 6–13: Ludi Apollinares

July 7: sacrifice to Consus

July 7: Nonae Caprotinae

July 7: festival of Pales

July 8: Vitulatio

July 15: Transvectio Equitum

July 17: dies natalis of the temple of Honos et Virtus

July 17: sacrifice to Victoria

July 18: dies ater (a black day)

July 19th and 21: Lucaria

July 20–30: Ludi Victoriae Caesaris

July 22: dies natalis of the temple of Concordia at the foot of the Capitoline

July 23: Neptunalia

July 25: Furrinalia

July 30: dies natalis of the temple of Fortuna Huiusce Diei

August 1: dies natalis of the temple of Spes (Hope) in the Forum Holitorium

August 3: Supplicia Canum (the Punishment of the Dogs)

August 5: festival of Salus

August 9: festival of Sol Indiges

August 12 and 13: festival of Hercules Invictus

August 13: festival of the Camenae

August 13: dies natalis of the temple of Castor and Pollux

August 13: Nemoralia

August 13: festival of Flora

August 13: dies natalis of the temple of Fortuna Equestris

August 13: dies natalis of the temple of Hercules Victor

August 13: festival of Vertumnus

August 17: Portunalia

August 19: Vinalia

August 21: Consualia

August 23: sacrifice to Maia during the Vulcanalia

August 23: sacrifice to the Nymphs in the Field during the Vulcanalia

August 23: sacrifice to Ops Opifera (Ops the Bringer of Help) during the Vulcanalia

August 24: festival of Luna

August 24: opening of the Mundus

August 25: Opiconsivia

August 27: Volturnalia

August 28: Games of Sol and Luna

September 1: festival of Jupiter Liber

September 1: festival of Juno Regina on the Aventine

September 1: offering to Jupiter Tonans (the Thunderer) on the Capitoline

September 5: dies natalis of the temple of Jupitor Stator

September 5–9: Ludi Romani

September 13: Epulum Jovis (Feast of Jupiter)

September 13: dies natalis of the temple of Jupiter Optimus Maximus

September 13: Epulum to Jupiter, Juno and Minerva

September 14: Equorum Probatio (the Approval of the Horses)

September 23: dies natalis of the rededication of the temple of Apollo

September 26: dies natalis of the temple of Venus Genetrix

October 1: festival of Fides

October 1: ceremony of the Tigillum Sororium

October 3–7: Bacchanalia

October 4: Ieiunnium Cereris

October 5: Opening of the Mundus

October 6: dies ater (a black day)

October 7: offering to Juno Curitis

October 7: offering to Jupiter Fulgur

October 9: sacrifices to Genius Publicus, Fausta Felicitas and Venus Victrix

October 10: dies natalis of the temple of Juno Moneta

October 11: Meditrinalia

October 12: Augustalia

October 13: Fontinalia

October 14: dies natalis of the temple of Di Penates

October 15: Capitoline Games

October 15: sacrifice of the October Horse to Mars

October 19: Armilustrium

October 26–November 1: Ludi Victoriae Sullanae

October 31–November 3: Festival of Isis

November 1: Ludi Circenses (end of the Ludi Victoriae Sullanae)

November 4–17: Ludi Plebeii (Plebeian Games)

November 8: Opening of the Mundus

November 13: festival of Feronia

November 13: festival of Fortuna Primigenia

November 13: Epulum Jovis

November 14: Equorum Probatio

December 3: Bona Dea Festival

December 5: festival of Faunus

December 8: festival of Tiberinus Pater

December 11: Agonalia for Jupiter Indiges

December 11: Septimontia, the Festival of the Seven Hills

December 12: dies natalis of the temple of Consus

December 13: Lectisternium for Ceres

December 13: dies natalis of the temple of Tellus

December 15: Consualia

December 17–23: Saturnalia

December 18: Eponalia

December 19: Opalia

December 21: Divalia, also called Angeronalia

December 22: dies natalis of the temple of the Lares Permarini

December 23: dies natalis of the temple of Juno Regina

December 23: dies natalis of the temple of the Tempestates

December 23: Sigillaria, the last day of Saturnalia

December 23: Larentalia

December 25: dies natalis of Sol Invictus

December 25: Brumalia

Januarius
January, a hollow month

J anuary is a resting time in the agricultural year. From the Winter Solstice to February seventh, there were few major tasks to be done on farms. The Kalends of January was the day when consuls took office for the year. The consulship was the highest office in the republic and there were two consuls each year. The year was usually referred to by the names of the two consuls, but in 59 BCE—technically the year of Julius and Bibulus—Julius Caesar so dominated his junior partner that it was referred to as the year of Julius and Caesar. As part of the process of taking office, the new consuls made vows and auspices.

The common people would begin the year with presents called *strenae*, which derives from the Sabine Goddess *Strenia*. The Sabines were a tribe of people in Latium with whom the earliest Romans intermarried, and some of the most prominent families from the Republican and Imperial periods were proudly Sabine in their heritage. The name Strenia might indicate strength or health. On the first day of the year, people would carry twigs from a grove sacred to Strenia to the citadel on the Capitoline hill.

There are four temple birthdays this month. Two on the Kalends are for the temples on the island in the Tiber. The shrine of Vica Pota celebrates its birthday on the fifth. A Latin Goddess of Victory, she eventually became syncretized with Victoria, the personification of victory. At the end of the month, the temple of Castor and Pollux marks its anniversary as well.

The sister of Castor and Pollux, Juturna, was associated with healing. Also called Diuturna, she was a water spirit of the River Numicus and might receive offerings during droughts. She had a sacred pool called the Lacus Juturnae near her brothers' temple as well as a temple of her own on the Campus Martius. Her festival on the eleventh of January was the same day as the anniversary of her temple.

Most of the festivals in this month are *stativae*, or fixed-date celebrations. The rural festival of Compitalia, however, is a *conceptiva*, a movable feast whose date was announced by the consuls after they took office each year. It could be held as early as December 17th or as late as January 5th, but was typically placed around January 3rd, which is the date given below. The Feriae Sementivae festival—also called the Paganalia—of Tellus and Ceres this month was another conceptiva. The fixed days of the month—the Kalends, Nones and Ides—are indicated below. Take note of the following dates:

1st of the month: the Kalends of Januarius

1st of the month: consuls took office and auspices were taken

1st of the month: dies natalis of the temple of Aesculapius

1st of the month: dies natalis of the temple of Vediovis

3rd of the month: Compitalia (moveable)

5th of the month: the Nones of Januarius

5th of the month: dies natalis of the shrine of Vica Pota

9th of the month: Agonalia of Janus

11th of the month: Juturnalia

11th and 15th of the month: Carmentalia

13th of the month: the Ides of Januarius

24th–26th of the month: Feriae Sementivae

27th of the month: Ludi Castores

27th of the month: dies natalis of the temple of Castor and Pollux

Dies Natalis of the Temples on the Tiber Island

At the beginning of the month are two *dies natalium* (birthdays) of temples on the island in the Tiber River that flows through the city of Rome. One is a temple of Aesculapius, a healing God of Greek origin, and the other a temple of Vediovis, a Roman deity who began as a God of swamps and volcanos but over time became associated with Jupiter as a chthonic and harmful version of him. He also eventually became associated with Apollo. Vediovis' preferred sacrifice was a female goat, in a rite called the *ritu humano*, which could mean that the sacrifice was being done on behalf of humans, particularly the dead, or that it was a stand-in for human sacrifice.

Rome absorbed most foreign cults through assimilation and syncretism, but some maintained their distinct identities even as they were officially accepted and brought into Rome. One of the tools for sanctioning new cults was to consult the Sibylline books. In the early days before the Romans overthrew their kings, Tarquinius Superbus (the proud) was the last monarch of Rome. An old woman came into town and gained an audience with the king, during which she offered him nine books for a set price. The king refused because the cost was exorbitant, so the old woman burned three of the books, and demanded the same price for the remaining six. Again he refused, so she burned three more and insisted he pay the same cost for the remaining three as she had originally asked for all nine. The king consulted his augurs, who told him that he should have bought the nine and that he should certainly pay the price for the remaining three. When the king acquired the books, they were taken to the temple of Jupiter on the Capitoline hill. Access to the books was carefully guarded as they were thought to contain information about the fate of Rome. They were consulted in times of crisis, and suggested remedies to deal with various threats. The Romans deeply valued tradition and to import a foreign cult was to risk compromising the religious fabric of the state. If the Sibylline books recommended that a new God be brought in, though, their very antiquity lent a legitimacy to the new cult that was unassailable.

One famous instance of the Romans consulting the books came in 293 BCE when a plague struck Rome. Following the oracle's advice, envoys set out for Epidauros, the site of the main temple of Asklepios—the healing God—in Greece. That temple sanctuary had sacred snakes and dogs that roamed freely, even interacting with worshippers who would sleep in the temple and be healed of their ailments. The Roman emissaries brought back a statue of the God—whose name they Latinized to Aesculapius—and one of the sacred serpents. The snake and the statue took up residence on an island in the Tiber River and the Romans dedicated a temple to Aesculapius in 291 BCE. That temple carried on the traditions of its mother cult in Epidaurus, keeping dogs and snakes and allowing the sick to incubate dreams in the temple for healing.

Asclepius, vintage illustration

Compitalia

The most revered of the *numina* were the Lares and Penates, venerated from ancient times and early in their history synonymous with ancestral ghosts. They were residing spirits, the embodiment of the family cult. Every Roman family had its own Lar, protector of the home, and several Penates, Gods of the hearth and guardians of the storeroom.

A niche held an icon of the Lar, prayed to each morning. It was a jaunty little bronze statuette, a youthful figure in a short tunic holding a dish and raising aloft a drinking horn. At mealtime, bits of food were burned in the dish as offerings to departed ancestors. In later years, perhaps to reinforce its powers, the shrine typically held two Lares with a central icon of Vesta, Goddess of the hearthfire and closely associated with the Penates.

At the time of family events—births, birthdays, weddings, safe returns from journeys, deaths—the Lares received special attention. The little icons were crowned, decked with garlands, and enjoyed offerings of incense, cakes, honey, wine and sometimes a pig.

Even preceding their ancient roles in the home, the spirits had worked their magic as protectors of towns. The Lares were presiding deities of shrines set up at the crossroads (compita,) where their spheres of influence extended to the surrounding areas—in archaic times, villages and towns and in the classical era, urban neighborhoods. In the earliest days, the shrines at the compita were set up during the festival of Compitalia with openings facing each road to a family farm. A wooden doll was placed within the shrine for each free member of the household, and a woolen ball for each slave. Sacrifices were held for the Lares within each home as well.

In Rome, the Lares guarded the state itself at a temple near the Palatine, and coins honored the Lares of State, with designs including lances and watchdogs. During the annual Compitalia, all the Lares—public and private—were lovingly honored and celebrated with community games.

The Compitalia was not a state festival until relatively late, but was certainly traditional, perhaps due to the more personal and private nature of the veneration of the Lares. The city of Rome was not economically segregated in the same way that modern cities have rich and poor neighborhoods. Typically, poorer families would live on the higher floors of buildings where the risk from fire was greater and wealthier families would dwell on the lower floors. The result was that shrines of the Lares at the crossroads were tended by rich and poor, slave and free alike.

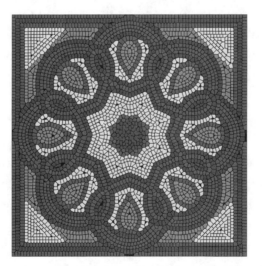

Agonalia of Janus

The first month of the modern calendar receives the protection of Janus, God of beginnings, developed from his supervision of entrances. On January 9, the residence of the *rex sacrorum* (high priest) in the Forum was the site of the annual state sacrifice to Janus—an offering of a ram. Romans believed his spirit hovered in all doorways, gates, and passageways. Since entrances also serve as exits and since good beginnings imply good endings, Janus is depicted *bifrons*—with two faces, handsome and bearded, for viewing forward and backward simultaneously.

All things at the center of the home were also sacred at the center of the city. Together with Vesta, Janus forms half of the essential parts of the home—the hearth (Vesta) and the door (Janus.) These two were invoked at the beginning and end of all prayers, sacrifices and religious rites. Romans especially sought the patronage of Janus for maintaining peace after war, purification of youths on the threshold of manhood and good luck in sowing the new crop.

A mythical king whose reign was a golden age and who was deified after his death, Janus' worship first existed as an ancient pre-Roman cult, later introduced to Rome by its founder, the legendary Romulus. Beyond these tales, though, even the ancient historians knew little of the origins of this most Roman of the Gods. His name is a masculine form of Diana, so they speculated that he may have been the Sun to her Moon, or perhaps the heavens themselves, the arc of the sky being akin to the arch of a gateway.

It is important to remember, though, that Janus does not just protect the doorway—he *is* the doorway just as Vesta is the flame as well as the Goddess of the hearth. He is also one of the oldest Gods—note his title "God of Gods" at the end of the fragment of archaic hymn below.

Carmen Saliare[1]

"You, the planter, the sower! I have bought all
things truly for you, the wide opener.
Now you are the spirit of the doorways, the
good oak, the good passage (Janus.)
You will come above all, you who are better
than those kings.
Sing to the father of the Gods, pray to the
God of Gods!
When you thunder, you God of the light, they
tremble before you."

—tr. Mab Borden

---

1   These lines are fragments of an archaic hymn in a form of Latin that was obscure to even the Romans in ancient times, and the meaning of some words is uncertain, as is the order of the lines. The first lines are addressed to Janus and the last line is most likely addressed to Jupiter.

Carmentalia

The two-day festival of Carmentalia is divided by a three-day interval, with celebrations on the eleventh and fifteenth of the month. There are a number of vague explanations for this arrangement—that the two festival days represented the Romans and the Sabines or that the festival was originally one day and a second day was added in response to some event—but none is certain.

The festival celebrated Carmenta, a name deriving from *carmen* meaning charm, song and prophecy. Indeed, Carmenta was a Goddess of prophecy who also had connections to childbirth. She was addressed by the titles Prorsa (feet first) and Postverta (head first,) the positions of babies in the birth canal. Her cult was tended primarily by women, but she did have her own flamen, and imposed a taboo on her worshippers that no leather be allowed in her temple.

Carmenta was a water nymph, a daughter of the River Ladon, and legend tells that she was the mother of Evander, an early settler in the area of Rome. She prophesied that he would be banished from his homeland and then she sailed with him to Italy. Before setting foot on the new land, she greeted its Gods, the nymphs and the spirits of its waters and prophesied that the Trojan hero Aeneas—the mythical ancestor of Romulus, Caesar and Augustus—would come to Latin shores.

Fasti

"When at once she had grasped in her mind the
divine fires,
she would produce from her truthful mouth

songs full of God.
She said that a disturbance approached her son
and herself,
and many things besides which in time turned
out to be true…

But the lucky seer while she lived was most
pleasing to the Gods
and as a Goddess possesses this day in the
month of Janus."

–Ovid, tr. Mab Borden

Feriae Sementivae

The farmers of Latium began their Autumn sowing at the equinox and continued until the Winter Solstice. At that point, they hung up their ploughshares and rested from their labors through the period of winter festivals until Spring sowing began again around February seventh. The last of these festivals is the Feriae Sementivae, which blesses the seed sown in Autumn, the crops that will burst forth in Spring and the unsown seed to be used in the spring planting which was about to begin.

This festival was also called the Paganalia, a name that indicates that it was celebrated in the *pagi*—small, rural farming communities. Originating in the countryside, this sowing festival was continued in the city even after most of the populace were no longer engaged in agriculture. The festival events depicted by Ovid describe practices best suited to the farm, but there could also have been worship of the festival's deities at their temples in the city.

Prayers for the seed were offered to Ceres, the Goddess of the grain crops and to Tellus—Earth. Ceres had her own priest, the Flamen Cerialis. In the fifth century BCE, the Sibylline books advised that the Romans associate her cult with the worship of the Greek Demeter and that they bring the worship of Demeter, Kore and Iacchus from Eleusis into Rome. These three Gods shared a temple on the Palatine Hill. Ceres was also purificatory—grain was sprinkled over the heads of sacrificial animals and a sacrifice to her cleansed homes after funerals.

At the Feriae Sementivae, the prayers to Ceres and Tellus thanked them for the gift of domesticated grains so that the people no longer had to eat acorns and entreated the Goddesses to protect the seed from all threats—from harsh weather, disease and hungry birds. Farmers hung garlands around the necks of their oxen and offered cakes to the Goddesses. On the second day, they sacrificed a pregnant sow to the pregnant Earth. They also hung *oscilla* from the trees—small masks and figurines which served as offerings. These would swing back and forth as the branches swayed in the breeze, giving Latin the verb *oscillare* (to swing) and English the word "oscillate."

Seated Demeter, vintage illustration

Fasti

"While the day of the rites is uncertain,
nevertheless the season is sure—
it's when the field is pregnant with the
sown grain.
Young bulls, stand wreathed with garlands at
your full stalls.
In the warm spring, your work will return!
Let the peasant hang up on its peg the
ploughshare that has discharged its service—
the soil recoils from any wound in the cold.
You overseer, give a rest to the Earth now that
the planting's done
and give a rest to the men who tended
the Earth.
Let the countryside have a festival! Farmers, go
around the countryside
and give the yearly offering cakes to the
country hearths.
Let the mothers of the crops, both
Tellus and Ceres,
be placated with their own grain, and with the
inner organs of a pregnant sow.
Ceres and Earth protect their
shared obligation:
one provides the crops with their source, the
other with their place.
Partners in the work, through whom the
ancient ways were improved,
and through whom the acorns of the oak were
conquered by more useful food,

satisfy the greedy farmers with a
boundless harvest,
so that they may reap gifts worthy of
their worship.
Give uninterrupted growth to the
tender seedlings
And do not let the new shoots be burned by
cold snow.
When we sow, clear the sky with gentle winds.
When it lies hidden, sprinkle the seed with
heavenly water.
And do not allow the flocks of birds bent on
harming the crops
to plunder the farmland of Ceres.
You also, ants, spare the sown grain.
After the harvest there will be plenty of
plunder for you.
For now, let grain grow free from
scaly mildew
and do not let it fade through the fault of
the weather
nor fail through withering,
or, too fertile, die from its own wanton
overgrowth.
Let the fields be free of poison darnel
damaging to the eyes,
and let fruitless reeds not spring up in the
cultivated ground.
May the field give back with enormous
interest the crops of wheat and the barley and
the spelt that must twice endure the fire.

This I hope for you, farmers! Hope it for
yourselves and let each Goddess bring about
these sure prayers.
For a long time wars held men captive. The
sword was more ready than the plough and
the ploughing bull conceded to the warhorse.
Hoes rested and mattocks turned into spears,
the helmet was fashioned from the weight of
the rake.
Thanks to the Gods and to your house!
For a long time now, wars lie tied up in chains
under your feet.
Let the ox come under the yoke and the seed
under the tilled Earth!
Peace nourishes Ceres—Ceres the nursling
of Peace."

—Ovid, tr. Mab Borden

Castor and Pollux

On the twenty-seventh day of January, the Romans celebrated the anniversary of a temple of Castor and Pollux and the nearby port city of Ostia held games in their honor—the Ludi Castores. Called the Dioscuri (sons of Zeus,) the twins were sons of Leda. The father of Pollux was Zeus while Leda's husband Tyndareus fathered Castor the horsebreaker, but in some tales they are both mortal, in others both divine and in yet more they share their immortality.

The most common legend tells that Zeus took the form of a swan to seduce lovely Leda and she also slept with her mortal husband on the same night. In time she gave birth to the two babes, one mortal and one immortal. Their names are woven through many legends, with the twins showing up as Argonauts, as hunters of the Calydonian boar in tales of Theseus and Helen. When Castor was killed in a fight, Pollux appealed to Zeus, who allowed him to share his immortality with his brother, each alternating days in the underworld and days on Olympus.

Although the Roman cult of the Dioscuri focused primarily on Castor, both twins were associated with horses, boxing and other athletic activities. The brothers would help sailors at sea—where they would show themselves in the form of St. Elmo's fire—and were often called upon by soldiers in grave distress on the battlefield.

Greek in origin, the twins came early into Roman worship and had many monuments throughout Rome. Although associated with the Greek cult, their worship was both ancient and widespread in the region— horse-associated divine twins figure in proto-Indo-European religion and might date as far back as the Neolithic period.

Februarius
February, a hollow month

S pring began on the seventh of this month with grain sowing. Farmers also began to prepare vineyards and olive and fruit groves for the growing season. The name of the month itself comes from the *februa*—a tool used for purification that shows up in the Lupercalia. That festival along with the Parentalia are the major feasts of the month, but there are numerous smaller rites as well as two moveable feasts.

On the Kalends are two observances—the *sacra* (rites) at the grove of Alernus and the anniversary of the temple of Juno Sospita. Alernus was an ancient and obscure God of his grove, who received sacrifices on this day. Along with Alernus, Ovid also mentions sheep sacrifices for Jupiter the Thunderer on the Kalends. Juno Sospita was an alternate name for Juno Sispes, meaning "savior." A protector of the state, she originated in the ancient Latin city of Lanuvium and the consuls of the Roman Republic would visit Lanuvium to make sacrifices to her before temples to her were constructed in Rome. This martial form of the Queen of the Gods is shown on coins with a chariot, shield and spear, and draped in a goatskin with horns still attached. She is associated with snakes and either crows or ravens.

The anniversary of the temple of Concordia—the personification of harmony—falls on the Nones of the month. The first of two festivals of Faunus falls on the Ides, with another festival for the rustic God in August. The Ides is also the beginning of the Parentalia, an ancestral festival lasting until the twenty-first and overlapping with the purificatory fertility rites of Lupercalia. The next day is the closely related festival of Caristia which celebrates the living family after honoring the ancestors. Two days later on the twenty-fourth is the Regifugium, which means "the flight of the king." This feast is an unlucky day that marks the overthrow of Tarquinius Superbus, the last tyrannical Roman king.

A moveable feast this month was the feast of the ovens—Fornacalia. Its latest date was February 17th, but was celebrated at different times by different groups of people within the city. The second moveable feast of the Amburbium fits with the purificatory trend of the month overall. This purification of the city involved a circumambulation of the city walls as well as prayers and sacrifices. Take note of the following dates:

1st of the month: the Kalends of Februarius

1st of the month: sacra at the grove of Alernus

1st of the month: dies natalis of the temple of Juno Sospita

5th of the month: the Nones of Februarius

5th of the month: dies natalis of the temple of Concordia

13th of the month: the Ides of Februarius

13th of the month: Festival of Faunus

13th–21st of the month: Parentalia

15th of the month: Lupercalia

17th of the month: Quirinalia, the Feast of the Fools

21st of the month: Feralia

22nd of the month: Carista

23rd of the month: Terminalia

24th of the month: Regifugium

27th of the month: Equirria

Moveable feast this month: Amburbium

Moveable feast before the 17th of the month: Fornacalia

Parentalia

The relations between the living and the dead—the *di manes*—were circumscribed by mutual obligations. Ancestors were, after all, still members of the family, and the Parentalia was a renewal of funeral rites that was duty as well as a time of personal memorial. On the anniversary of a person's death, their heir was obliged to process to the tomb to tend to it, cover it with flowers and make offerings. These could include honey, milk, oil, wine and the blood of black animals, which was preferred for the dead. The traditional words, "*salve, sancte parens*" (hail, venerable parent) were spoken, and then the living would dine with dead. At this time, people could ask their ancestors for whatever they needed, but especially good luck. The rites of the Parentalia followed this same pattern. Families would travel to the necropolis outside the city to make offerings and then feast at the tombs of their dead ancestors.

Although most of the observances of Parentalia were private, family affaris, on the Ides of February, which was the first day of the festival, a Vestal led the collective rites for the ancestors of Rome. These were held at the tomb of the Vestal Tarpeia, who famously betrayed Rome in the earliest days of the monarchy, just after the city was founded. Rome was under siege by the Sabines, and Tarpeia snuck into the Sabine camp, offering to let the enemy in, asking only that they give her what they wore on their left arms. They agreed, and after she opened the gates, instead of the bracelets and jewelry she expected, all the Sabine soldiers threw on her their shields, which were carried on the left arm. The great weight of them crushed her to death, as befits a traitor. Her body was thrown from the Capitoline hill at a place called the Tarpeian Rock after her, and where traitors were executed down all the centuries after.

Tarpeia may have been a traitor, but she was nonetheless one of the ancestors of the state and so she was included in the Parentalia. This festival propitiated the spirits, both the honored dead and those hostile to the individual, family or state. The living had nothing to fear from the dead, provided all their obligations were fulfilled. Ovid says that the spirits of the dead are not greedy and require only simple offerings, but he offers a warning as well, telling of a time when the rites of the Parentalia were neglected during a war. The ancestors rose out of their grave and wandered through the city while spirits howled in the nearby fields.

The Parentalia was not considered an unlucky (*nefas*) time, but because spirits were about, officials did not wear the insignia of their offices, temples were closed and there could be no marriages during the entire festival. The Feralia on the twenty-first, though, was labelled as unlucky in some calendars because the ghosts were wandering the city eating the food put out for them. This public festival for the dead constituted the last day of Parentalia.

The Feralia was also a day for a strange womens' rite of the Silent Goddess. This deity was a nymph named Lara who refused to comply with Jupiter's instructions to block her sister Juturna from fleeing him when he wanted to rape her. She warned her sister and even went to Juno to tell her of her husband's plans. Enraged, Jupiter ordered that she be shut up beneath the Earth with the manes, to become the nymph of an underworld lake. She became enamored of the God sent to drag her down to that realm of shadows and bore him twins who became the Lares, the protectors of the home.

To perform the rituals of the Silent Goddess on the Feralia, an old woman would gather the young girls of the family around her. Using three fingers, she would place three pieces of incense into a mousehole under the threshold of the house. Then she would fasten a charmed thread with lead, roll seven black beans around in her mouth, and take the head of a small fish which she had sealed up with pine pitch and pierced with a bronze pin and place it in the fire. Lastly, she would pour wine onto the fish's head and give some to the girls, although she drank most of it herself. When this rite was finished, she'd instruct the young women, saying "we've fastened closed the mouths of our enemies and their unfriendly tongues."

The very next day was the Carista, a celebration of love within the living family. Not unlike a family reunion, it gathered together the living after the collective honoring of the dead. At this feast, the Lares of the family were honored and received a share of the sacred meal.

Fasti

"A tile covered with spread out garlands
is enough,
and scattered fruits and a scant grain of salt,
and Ceres (grain) softened with wine and
scattered violets.
Let a clay pot hold these, left in the middle of
the road.

. . .

Even by these things is a ghost able to
be pacified.
When the fire of an altar has been set up, add
prayers and your own words."

—Ovid, tr. Mab Borden

Lupercalia

The tale of Rome begins on the hills of the Turkish coast and in the halls of Olympus where lovely Venus took great delight in causing the immortal Gods to carry on their many affairs with humans. Goddesses looked with favor on mortal men and Gods took mortal women into their beds. Jupiter began to fear that Venus was secretly laughing at them all and decided to play the same game upon her. He put into her gracious heart a fierce desire for the shepherd Anchises, a cousin of King Priam of Troy. In her temple on Cyprus Venus bathed in fragrant oils and dressed herself in gold, and then departed to find the herder tending his flocks. As she crossed Mount Ida to find him, the wild beasts followed her. Wolves and lions, bears and leopards— all were seized with lust and began to mate in the shadow of the mountain, so potent was the presence of the Goddess. When she came upon Anchises at last, he knew she was no mortal woman and asked what Goddess she might be. He promised to build her an altar, whoever she was, and asked her blessing. She laughed and spun a tale for him that she was a mortal girl who had been playing in the fields with Diana and her nymphs when Mercury swept her away and carried her to Mount Ida, telling her she was to be the wife of Anchises, and she promised that her father would send a dowry as soon as the message reached him.

Anchises' yearning for her was so overwhelming that he believed her and led her by the hand to the pile of furs on which he slept and she went with downcast eyes, feigning the unease of a virgin. Afterwards, she clothed herself in the raiment of a Goddess while he slumbered and then woke him, showing herself in a truer form.

Venus

It was his turn to avert his eyes and he begged her to have mercy on him because all the stories said that a man who slept with a Goddess was never well afterwards. She reassured him that he would come to no harm, but confessed her embarrassment should anyone discover that she had mated with a mortal, and revealed her plan to conceal it. She would give to the nymphs the child she would soon bear him, and he would be raised by them until he was five, when she would bring him to his father. The child would be as beautiful as the immortal Gods, so she made him promise to tell anyone who asked that the child was the son of one of the mountain nymphs rather than an immortal Goddess. If he confessed the boy's true parentage, she told him, he would feel the searing pain of Jupiter's thunderbolt in the moment he became ash. Anchises swore to keep their liaison secret and promised to uphold her story and the Goddess departed to Olympus.

When their son Aeneas arrived, he was indeed godlike, and he became a great hero as befits the son of Venus. He was handsome, strong and capable in battle, but the Romans called him Pious Aeneas—meaning that he was both loyal and dutiful—a virtue central to Roman identity. A second cousin of the royal house of Troy, he married the princess Creusa and contended against the Greeks in the great war. Aeneas faced Achilles in one to one combat, although even a child of a Goddess was no match for the great hero. On the night the city fell, the ghost of his cousin Hector appeared to Aeneas and warned him to escape across the sea. Aeneas instead stayed and tried to defend the city. Driven back with the rest of the Trojans to the palace, he witnessed the slaughter of King Priam and only then did he see that the fight was lost. Trying to save whom he could, Aeneas had to beg his father Anchises to join him, and even then the old shepherd refused until a sign from the Gods convinced him. Realizing his wife was lost when he saw Creusa's ghost, Aeneas carried his aged father on his back and led his young son Ascanius by the hand as they fled the burning city, leading those few Trojans who could escape to the sea.

After six years of wandering the Mediterranean in search of a new home, Juno sent a storm which washed them up on the shores of Carthage in North Africa. They rested there for a year, and Aeneas had an ill-fated love affair with Queen Dido until Mercury came to remind him that his fate lay elsewhere, and he slipped out of Carthage by night. When Dido learned that he had left, she took her life with a sword she had once gifted to her lover. After leaving Carthage, Aeneas eventually made his way to the shores of central Italy and sailed up the Tiber River to Latium, where the King Latinus welcomed him and the other Trojan warriors. The king's daughter Lavinia was engaged to another King named Turnus, but Aeneas challenged Turnus for the girl's hand. In marrying Lavinia, Aeneas joined the royal bloodline of Troy with that of the Latins, founding a new dynasty.

Among the scions of this new line was Numitor, the good king of the city of Alba Longa. The legend tells that his wicked brother Amulius usurped Numitor's throne, killing all of Numitor's sons. Amulius let his niece Rhea Silvia live but forced her into chastity by consecrating her to the maiden Goddess Vesta. Unable to resist her great beauty and unwilling to let such injustice go unchecked, the God Mars slept with her in secret and when her pregnancy became known, Amulius locked Rhea Silvia away. When her twin sons Romulus and Remus were born, the king ordered his servants to throw the babes into the Tiber River. There had been so much rain and flooding that Spring, though, that the usurper's servants couldn't make it to the banks of the river, so instead they left the twins to die beneath a tree on the Palatine Hill. In another version of the tale, Amulius feared the miasma that comes from slaying kin with bloodshed, so he ordered a servant to kill the babes by burying them alive, by exposure or by drowning. He didn't have the heart to carry it out directly, so the servant threw the basket with the babies into the Tiber. There the river God Tibernus calmed his waters and guided the basket to catch in the roots of a fig tree that dangled down into the water at the base of the Palatine.

In all versions of the story, a mother wolf happened by and began to suckle the babes, keeping them alive until they were discovered by Amulius' shepherd, Faustulus. The kind herder and his wife raised the children as shepherds. In some versions they disclosed to the boys their true identity when they became young men, and the noble twins killed the fiend Amulius and restored Numitor to his throne. In other versions, Remus got into a fight with some of Amulius' shepherds, was arrested and dragged before the king and Romulus and some friends came to rescue him, killing the usurper in the process. However it came about, their identity was revealed, and Numitor regained his position. Like Aeneas, Romulus and

Remus were pious and would not unseat their grandfather from his place, but they were also unwilling to wait for their inheritance, so the twins set out to found a city of their own.

They had a disagreement about the site for their city—Remus favored the Aventine Hill while Romulus preferred the Palatine, the very area near the Tiber where the good shepherd Faustulus had found them. Romulus and Remus began to argue and looked to the sky for a sign of whose part the Gods would take. The

The she-wolf suckling the twins
Romulus and Remus

omens were unclear, though, with Remus seeing six birds first and Romulus seeing twelve. Romulus began to build the wall of his city despite the disagreement, but Remus was still bitter from the quarrel and jumped over the low barrier to make fun of it. Romulus trucks him over the head with his spade, killing him, and declared that the same fate would meet any who dared to breach the walls of Rome.

So say the legends. Historically, Alba Longa was an ancient city in Latium in central Italy. Its exact location is unclear but there are villages and towns in the region that date to around the first millennium BCE, aligning with the probable date of the fall of Troy. Whether there was ever a Trojan War at all is uncertain, but it is likely that there was a conflict in that region a few hundred years before the Homeric epics were written down, even if it was not as grand as the legends that surround it. In historical times, many prominent Roman families traced their ancestry to Alba Longa, including the Julii who claimed descent through Aeneas to Venus herself. For this reason, Julius Caesar, his great-nephew and adopted son Augustus and their heirs in the Julio-Claudian dynasty of emperors used dolphins, seashells, Cupids and other Venus-associated imagery in their portraits—to remind everyone else that they were, in some small measure, divine.

The ancient Romans offered worship to Quirinus—the deified Romulus—at the *casa Romuli*, a round hut with thatched roof and wattle and daub walls on a slope of the Palatine Hill that was supposed to be the house he shared with his foster parents. It caught fire several times. Another sacred site associated with the founding of the city was the *Lupercal*, the cave of the wolf that suckled the young twins. Also located on the Palatine, the Luperci priests of Faunus celebrated the Lupercalia there for over a thousand years.

In the festival, the Romans gathered at the Lupercal where the Luperci—a name meaning "wolf-men"—offered cakes and sacrificed a dog and goats. Then two patrician boys of noble blood would step forward. The Luperci touched the boys' foreheads with the bloody knives, and then others wiped off the blood with scraps of wool soaked in milk and the boys laughed. Perhaps in doing this, the boys became Romulus and Remus, the noble twins who were sentenced to death but saved by the nourishment of the wolf. Afterwards, they cut the skins of the sacrificed goats into strips called *februa* and ran naked through the city—wearing only februa strips as belts—striking anyone in their paths with the februa. Plutarch wrote that this circuit of the city reenacted the celebratory race of the companions of Romulus and Remus who sprinted to the Lupercal in celebration once they had defeated Amulius. He also said it was reminiscent of a prayer of Romulus and Remus to Faunus to replenish their flocks in a difficult year when they were still shepherds because following their prayer, they ran to find their flocks and were naked so that their sweat wouldn't bother them. He also suggested that the dog sacrifice was an offering to the nourishing wolf herself. Whatever the origin of the ancient rites, purification by the februa was thought to help a woman conceive, and so those hoping for a child would throw themselves in the path of the Luperci.

By starting at the Lupercal, these ceremonies were deeply tied to the founding myths of Rome and maintaining the festival remained an important obligation of the state throughout Rome's history. Enacting the festival annually ensured the safety and prosperity of Rome. Its origins and meaning were so obscure, though, that under Augustus the Romans invented a God named Lupercus for the festival, whom they said must be the protector of shepherds and in whose honor they must have been holding the Lupercalia down all those centuries. There was a great deal of revelry and the festival was so popular that in Christian times, the church had difficulty putting a stop to it, perhaps especially because its precise connection to the Gods had always been so unclear that Christians might not have felt too badly about it. At the end of the fifth century, Pope Gelasius I finally settled on transforming the ancient purification festival on the 15th of February into a feast of the purification of the virgin Mary. He faced resistance from the Roman nobility, though, who were by that time all Christian. They argued that foregoing the Lupercalia festival would bring calamities to the city—plagues, failed harvests and wars—and that the Byzantines in the East would overtake them in wealth and prominence, which, of course, they did.

Life of Romulus

"Two youths of noble birth run,
smiting all those whom they meet,
as once with brandished weapons,
down from Alba's heights,
Remus and Romulus ran."

–Plutarch, tr. Bernadotte Perrin, 1914

Quirinalia

Quirinus was an ancient Sabine war deity and possibly a cult title of Mars. His veneration on the Quirinal Hill predated the founding of Rome. He had his own flamen—the flamen Quirinalis—who was one of the three greater flamens. He had a temple on the Quirinal with two myrtles growing before it, named the patrician and the plebeian, suggesting balance and harmony within the state. He was one of the original three Gods of the Capitoline triad along with Jupiter and Mars in the archaic period, but these gave way over time to Jupiter, Juno and Minerva.

Quirinus is also the name used to refer to Romulus, the legendary founder of Rome, after he died and became a God. After a long rule of thirty-seven years in which he founded the city, absorbed the neighboring Sabines into it and fought numerous battles to defend Rome, Romulus was succeeded by the Sabine Numa Pompilius, the king who established many Roman religious traditions. The kingship was not inherited—Numa was elected by the senate. How exactly Romulus, however, died is unclear. The legend goes that one day Romulus simply disappeared in a cloud of dust, which ancient historians interpreted to mean either that Mars had taken him up into the heavens or that he had been stabbed to death by his own senators—perhaps both. Romulus was deified and his cult and that of Quirinus became the same. Romulus was one of only seven kings of early Rome and the senate was a political body to be reckoned with from the earliest days. This festival is also called the Feast of Fools, with the only slight explanation having to do with the Fornacalia rather than the Quirinalia. Roman skepticism and piety were close bedfellows, so perhaps it was considered foolish to believe every in legend, even when tradition demanded an outward show of devotion.

Fornacalia
the Feast of the Ovens

This moveable feast was held at different times by each *curia* (a religious and political grouping of the people.) This festival involved offerings at the ovens in private homes as well as rites in each curia. The date for each curia to celebrate Fornacalia was posted publicly, but apparently most people celebrated it toward the end of the month. In the home, farro was roasted and crushed, then baked into cakes, and these were brought to the curia for a communal meal.

One sacrificial cake recipe from Cato the Elder dating to around 200 BCE calls for mixing two pounds of cheese (likely similar to cream cheese) and a pound of flour with an egg and then baking it slowly at a low temperature on leaves near a warm hearth. He recommends only using half a pound of flour if you prefer a lighter texture. The ingredients and gentle baking method are similar to a modern cheesecake, so see below for for a version of this recipe that is usable in a modern kitchen. You can use the cake as an offering for this or any other festival.

SACRIFICIAL CAKE

1 ½ lbs (three 8 oz blocks) cream cheese, at room temperature
8 oz cheddar, asiago or other cheese at room temperature OR another 8 oz cream cheese
3 ¾ cups flour OR 1 ¾ for the lighter amount
1 egg, at room temperature
1 tsp salt (optional)

Cream the cheeses together (they must be at room temperature or they won't blend!) Lightly beat the egg to avoid incorporating too much air into the cake (it could crack,) then mix in thoroughly with the cheese mixture. Cato does not call for salt, but the flavor will be improved by adding a teaspoon to the flour at this point. Gently stir the flour into the cheese mixture. Generously grease the bottom and sides of a nine-inch springform pan, then sprinkle with bread crumbs. Pour the batter into the pan. To mimic Cato's long, slow baking time, bake your cake at 200 degrees Fahrenheit for six to eight hours. You can also bake at 325 degrees in a water bath for an hour and 15 minutes to an hour and 30 minutes. If you use the water bath method, wrap the outside of the pan—bottom and sides—in a double layer of aluminum foil to avoid leakage. Place the cake pan in a larger pan with high sides such as a casserole dish. Preheat the oven and boil a kettle of water. Place the casserole dish with the cake pan on the oven rack, then carefully pour the boiling water into the casserole dish to a depth of at least 1 ½ inches (but do not let the cake float.) Whichever method you use, at the end of the baking time the cake should be set but still jiggle in the middle only. When it is done, turn the oven off and leave the cake in the oven. Prop the oven door open a crack with the handle of a wooden spoon and allow to cool down over several hours. Refrigerate the finished cake.

Bakery in Pompeii, vintage illustration

Terminalia

February 23 marked the end of the ancient Roman year when the calendar began in March. Likewise, *termini* were boundary markers that signified the end of your land. On acquiring property, the boundary stones or sometimes posts were put in place with an ancient ritual: The householder or farmer dug a hole, set up an altar and lit a fire. An animal was sacrificed and its blood poured into the hole, along with fruit, wine, incense and honey, followed by the sacrificial ashes. Then the stone was anointed, covered with garlands, and fixed into the ground through the hot ashes. This ceremony marked the stones as *numina*. In later years these stones evolved into the household God Terminus, sometimes honored along with the Lares and Penates.

At the Terminalia in the countryside, adjacent neighbors gathered and each household placed garlands on their own side of the stone. Members of the family had specific roles in the ceremony and onlookers wore white garments. After the garlands hand been laid, the celebrants set up an altar with fire which was carried from the hearth by the farmers' wives. An old man cut up twigs and arranged them into a structure to kindle the fire. A small boy held a basket of dry bark to be used as kindling. A young daughter shakes three offerings of grain into the fire and also offers honey cakes. There was also wine and later a lamb and suckling pig were sacrificed, their blood sprinkled on the stone and their flesh consumed in the feast. The occasion concluded with songs and other diversions, joined by all members of the two families.

In the city, the feast was marked with sacrifices at a boundary stone which was set up in the temple of Jupiter Optimus

Maximus (the best and greatest.) When that temple was built, the Gods who were already being worshipped on the Capitoline had to be moved. The augurs were consulted to ensure that no God would take offense and every God agreed—except Terminus. This was interpreted in the best possible light: he had no intention of abandoning Rome and his cult would endure through the ages. Since he refused to move, however, the boundary stone at which Terminus was worshipped was incorporated into the new temple and honored thereafter each year at his festival.

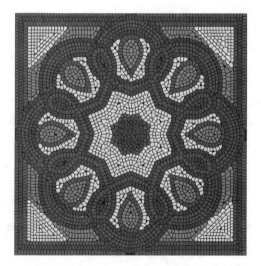

Equirria

Multiple annual Equirria celebrations honored horses, the superbly trained auxiliary of Roman military power. The festivals were under the rule of contentious Mars and a prelude to a season of war. During an Equirria, huge crowds converged on Rome to cheer the charioteers racing the perilous track at the Circus Maximus. The Circus accommodated 250,000 spectators in marble seats on the lower levels for patricians and in wooden seats for plebeians. The course was rounded so tightly that charioteers required immense skill to prevent spilling at each turn.

In the center of the track was the *spina*—literally the spine—consisting of two fenced areas with ceremonial figures used for marking laps. These were seven bronze dolphins with water pouring from their mouths and seven wooden eggs. At each lap, an official would reverse a dolphin and take down one egg so spectators could keep count of the contest. Between each fenced area stood two officials holding the winner's palm and wreath of victory for inspiration. Outside the fence, an *agitator* whipped the horses as they flashed by, and a *sparsor* threw water on the horses to keep them cool.

Most were two horse and four horse chariots performing a program of twenty-four races. The charioteers were often slaves held in high regard for their mastery of the sport. Occasionally the chariot races mixed with *desultores*, contests of riders each having two horses and leaping from one to the other around the track.

Races were the main event, but the preliminaries provided plenty of diversion. Their ceremony often began with a *pompa*—a gala procession in which images of the Gods were trundled in carts drawn by horses, mules or elephants, attended by priests and sometimes by the emperor himself seated in a chariot. Acrobats and clowns added their rowdy pleasures and brass bands added their clamor. Then the presiding official tossed a white flag onto the track—and the chariots were off, thundering, sparking, toppling!

Martius
March, a full month

This was the first month of the year for much of Roman history. Even when the new year was shifted to January, March still held a special significance—following the month of purification festivals in February, March began the military and agricultural years in earnest. The start of Spring may have been in February, but its verdant power was much more visible in March as the fields and vines began greening and growing. March was also strongly associated with the God Mars. Indeed, the name of the month, *mensis Martius*, simply means "the month of Mars." Other Gods also had months named for them, but none were as celebrated in their months as Mars was in his. He was particularly significant in the history of Rome and was a special patron of the city.

The month opens with a festival of Mars and the anniversary of his temple, as well as the Matronalia celebration, which honored his mother Juno Lucina. This title indicates her role as a Goddess of childbirth, as she brings children into the light. Every Kalends was sacred to her, but she was especially honored on the first Kalends of the year, so over time, March 1st became the date of her festival even after the new year itself moved to January. She had a temple on the Esquiline Hill and at this festival, women were forbidden from wearing knots of any kind. Belts were forbidden and they wore their hair unbound, which was unusual. Women would also receive gifts from family members on the Matronalia, and would prepare the family's meal for the day. On other days, this duty was typically reserved for slaves, but they were given the day of Matronalia off from work.

The new year of the old calendar, the Kalends was also the day when the sacred flame of Vesta was renewed each year. On this day the Salii warrior priests began their procession through Rome. On the Nones, the temple of Vediovis on the Capitoline Hill celebrated its anniversary, and on the 14th was the second Equirria festival. The first was in February and this second festival, while largely the same, fits in well with the martial character of the month as a parade of the cavalry is a demonstration of readiness for war.

Two holidays fall on the Ides—the first of five feasts of Jove in the year as well as a festival for a little-known Goddess called Anna Perenna. She is generally considered a personification of the year but the poet Ovid gave several possible mythological origins to explain the feast. Her festival placement on the 15th reveals its antiquity, though—it was originally the first Full Moon of the year, when the months began on the New Moon. Anna Perenna received both public and private sacrifices on this date.

For two days on the sixteenth and seventeenth of the month, the Romans engaged in a rite so ancient that its meaning was lost by the classical era. If there were any specific Gods being propitiated, that information has been lost. The ritual consisted of carrying small human figures made of reeds which were bound at the hands and feet. These were paraded through the city and made stops at twenty-seven shrines in the oldest parts of Rome. On the Ides of May, the whole ceremony was repeated, this time involving the Flamen Dialis. The May procession ended at the Tiber river, where thirty of these effigies were cast into the water by Vestal Virgins.

The Agonalia on the 17th was another rite in honor of Mars in this month of military festivals, but it may also have been part of the Liberalia on the same day. This was the time when boys took on the *toga virilis*—the toga of manhood—and subsequently enlisted for military service. The connection to the Gods of the Liberalia is not immediately apparent, and so it might be part of the Agonalia or the timing might be more closely related to the month as a whole belonging to Mars.

Two days after the Liberalia, the city celebrated the Quinquatria in honor of Minerva. On the last day of that festival, the final military display occurred on the twenty-third with the Tubilustrium, a purification of the trumpets. The instruments were themselves used in other purification rites, so this may have been a cleansing of ritual trumpets rather than military ones. The ceremony was repeated in May as well. The month ends with the dies natalis of the temple of Luna (the Moon) on the 31st. Take note of the following dates:

1st of the month: the Kalends of Martis

1st of the month: Feriae Martis and dies natalis of Mars

1st of the month: Matronalia

7th of the month: the Nones of Martis

7th of the month: dies natalis of the Temple of Vediovis (Capitoline)

14th of the month: Equirria

15th of the month: the Ides of Martis

15th of the month: Festival of Anna Perenna

15th of the month: Feriae Iovi

16th–17th of the month: procession of the Argei

17th of the month: Agonalia of Mars

17th of the month: Liberalia

19th of the month: Quinquatria

23rd of the month: Tubilustrium

31st of the month: dies natalis of the Temple of Luna

Feriae Martis

Feriae Martis

One ancient author gives March 1st as the birthday of the God, but whether or not this was the case, this was certainly a significant festival for him. Fresh laurels were laid out at the curiae and the regia (a dwelling of the pontifex maximus) as well as at the homes of the flamens. The twelve Salii warrior priests would perform their famous leaping dances with songs so ancient that the meaning of some words was not even clear to the Romans of the classical period, although they used "Mamuri" as an alternate name for Mars. These priests were chosen from among patricians who had both parents still living.

The story goes that the shield of Mars fell to Earth on the first day of this month. Copies of the God's shield were made and in commemoration, each March 1 the twenty-four Salii would carry their shields in a procession through the city—dancing, leaping and banging short spears against their shields for percussion to accompany their songs. Dressed in embroidered tunics with helmets and breastplates, they also carried swords. This dancing procession took place over a series of days, and each night the Salii would stop and rest in a different place, hanging up their weapons and holding a great feast.

When the Romans encountered Greek religion, for the most part they absorbed the myths and characteristics of the Greek Gods into their understanding of the Latin and Etruscan Gods they already worshipped. The result is a casual syncretism in which Jupiter is Zeus, Minerva is Athena, etc. The correlation is not perfect, though, and the Roman Gods maintained some of their own character. This is particularly noticeable in the differences between the Greek Ares, who is exclusively a deity of war, and the Roman Mars who is an agricultural God as well as a military one. The Greeks considered Ares to be a son of Zeus and Hera, and his martial power was destructive. He was generally regarded in Greece the way war was—as something you might need from time to time but which was not desirable in and of itself. Mars, on the other hand, was a bountiful patron who blessed the Romans with the gift of war, that is, with peace. From their perspective, the presence of a strong military power within a region brought an end to constant intertribal warfare, so the Romans regarded the power of Mars as a stabilizing force. There is a parallel in Roman history as well—the might of Augustus (who was not himself a general but nevertheless won wars by gaining the loyalty of the best military minds) brought an end to civil war and ushered in the Pax Romana—the Roman Peace—a golden age of art, architecture and literature in Rome.

In Greece, Ares was considered the son of Zeus and Hera, while lame Hephaestus is the son of Hera alone. In Rome, one version of the birth of Mars tells that he was the son of Juno apart from Jupiter. Flora, the Goddess of flowers, gave Juno a magical flower and the touch of its petals rendered the Queen of the Gods pregnant, demonstrating the connection of Mars to the verdant and fecund forces of nature. Indeed, Mars was worshipped as an agricultural God who protected the fields before he took on the martial characteristics of Ares.

Mars had his own flamen—the flamen Martialis—as well as a shrine on the Campus Martius and temples in several places in the city where he received sacrifices of boars, rams and bulls together. Only Mars, Apollo and Neptune among all the Gods could have bulls offered to them. The woodpecker was sacred to Mars along with the wolf, that ancient symbol of the Roman people. The prayer below addressing Mars with the reduplicated name Marmar and calling upon him as an invocation for aid in the Spring comes from an inscription and is one of the oldest prayers to the God that remains in existence.

Hymn of the Arval Priests

"Lares, come to our aid!

Lares, come to our aid!

Lares, come to our aid!

Marmar, do not let plague ruin or rain befall us!

Marmar, do not let plague ruin or rain befall us!

Marmar, do not let plague ruin or rain befall us!

Be fully satisfied, ferocious Mars! Jump over the
threshold, stand firm, strike!

Be fully satisfied, ferocious Mars! Jump over the
threshold, stand firm, strike!

Be fully satisfied, ferocious Mars! Jump over the
threshold, stand firm, strike!

He in turn will invoke all the spirits of the seed!

He in turn will invoke all the spirits of the seed!

He in turn will invoke all the spirits of the seed!

Marmor, come to our aid!

Marmor, come to our aid!

Marmor, come to our aid!

Triumph! Triumph! Triumph! Triumph!

Triumph!"

—tr. Mab Borden

Anna Perenna

On the Ides was the festival of Anna Perenna, held in her sacred grove. Because the origin of the Goddess was unclear in ancient times, Ovid gives several accounts of the possibilities. In one tale, the Trojan Aeneas had left his home, following his destiny to found a great new empire in the West. He tarried for a while in Carthage with Queen Dido, and when their love affair ended and he sailed on to Italy, she took her own life. The Numidians immediately attacked the now leaderless Carthage, and their king Iarbas conquered the city and took Dido's palace. Before the fallen queen's sister Anna fled, she made sure to complete Dido's funeral rites, tears mixing with perfumed oils as she made her final libations and cut a lock of her hair to leave in her sister's urn. Then she slipped out of the palace to the docks and found a ship to carry her away. She feared not only the conqueror Iarbas but also her cruel and ambitious brother Pygmalion, who had already proved his ruthlessness when he killed their brother-in-law.

Anna went first to the island of Melite in the Libyan Sea. Its king received her graciously but was unable to defend Anna when Pygmalion came looking for her. So she fled again, this time aiming for an obscure little region called Camere—a place her brother would never think to look. She was close to her destination when the sea rose up against her, battering the ship with waves and Notus the South Wind blew the ship off course. In one final blast, the storm drove the ship ashore on the coast of Latium in Italy, where Aeneas had married into the royal family, taking Lavinia as his wife.

Aeneas found Anna wandering the shore, and together they wept for Dido and the cruelty of fate. He brought her to his house and introduced her to Lavinia, expecting his wife to kindly receive his guest and old friend. Indeed, she was cordial—outwardly—in no small part due to the rich gifts Anna had brought on the ship from Carthage. But Lavinia was suspicious that any woman should have some familiarity with her husband, and wondered what other things were being given to him in secret. And so she began to plot against her own houseguest.

That night, the shade of Dido came to her sister. Standing at the foot of her bed—still covered in blood as Anna had last seen her—she screamed for her sister to run. Anna heeded the warning and fled through the window, hair loose and in her nightgown, running by moonlight over the fields. She came to the river Numicius who hid her safe beneath his waves. She pledged to become a nymph of the river, and took the name Perenna in honor of the perennial waters. Aeneas and his household wandered all over the fields looking for her, but her footsteps stopped at the riverbank.

At her festival in March, the common people gathered to picnic on the banks of the Tiber, and then they pitched tents and camped out there. It was said that you could predict the length of your life by the number of cups of wine you consumed, so it was a festival of drinking and the more, the better! There was dancing and singing of popular or even coarse songs rather than hymns and girls let their hair be undone. When all the festivities had ended, finally the participants would all stagger home, where they were called the Blessed Ones.

Liberalia

The tale goes that before the birth of Liber the vine planter, the hearths of altars were cold and shrines so neglected that they were covered with grass. Liber himself first set out fruits and grains on the altar of Jupiter. He offered cinnamon and incense to his father and processed with a bull whose entrails he roasted on the altar for the Gods. He invented libations and cakes, establishing these as sacrifices. He chose cakes in particular as his own offering, because he loves sweet things and was even the first to discover honey. One day, he was travelling with his satyr companions when the weapons they carried clanged together. The sound attracted bees, who began to swarm around them. Liber collected the bees and shut them in a hollow tree trunk, where they produced honey, which the God and his satyrs loved the instant they tasted it.

Another time, the God's companion—that old bald-headed Silenus—heard a buzzing sound near an old elm tree that was rotted out. Slowly and slyly, he led his donkey to it, casually pretending he hadn't heard anything so as not to alarm the bees. When he was close enough, he leaned against the bark and began looking for the honey that must be hidden in the hollow trunk. Instead of bees, though, hornets swarmed out, stinging his bare head and his face. He fell to the ground and in the chaos was kicked by his own donkey! He shouted to his sons, the satyrs, to help him, and they came running—only to laugh at his new limp and his swollen face. Liber laughed, too, and he showed the old man how to use mud to soothe the stings. But Liber loves honey and so the sweet, shining stuff is poured on cakes offered to him.

There are few accounts of the details of the Liberalia festival, but one account describes old women crowning themselves in garlands of ivy. These were called *sacerdotes Liberi*—priests of Liber. They made honey cakes and then set themselves up in the streets, each sitting next to a small altar. The sacerdotes sold the cakes along with oil to passersby, who would immediately sacrifice their wares at the little braziers.

This was the festival of Liber Pater, the Free Father, God of fertility and wine. He was an old Latin God whose worship was established in the area that would become Rome long before Greek cults were brought in. Jupiter is sometimes called Jupiter Liber, and Liber is also sometimes identified with the Carthaginian healing God Shadrapa.

Liber's cult was focused on the Aventine Hill, where he shared a temple with Ceres and Libera, a name which is simply a feminine equivalent of his own. The festival Liberalia may celebrate Libera as much as Liber. When the Sibylline books recommended that the Romans bring the Eleusinian deities into Rome, they explicitly connected Ceres with Demeter, Libera with Kore and Liber with Iacchos—a name of Dionysus used in the Eleusinian Mysteries. The influence flowed two ways, though, as Liber also became an epithet of Dionysus.

While there is no reason through most of Roman history to connect this particular festival with the phallic Greek rites of Dionysus, the Christian St. Augustine in the 4th century CE derided this celebration with a description reminiscent of the Dionysia and other Greek Festivals of the wine God. He said that a large phallus was processed through the fields and then through the streets of the city, and that it was accompanied by obscene songs.

Quinquatria

The oldest parts of the Quinquatria involved the purification of the shields of the Salian priests of Mars, but over time the festival became associated with Minerva because one of her temples had its dies natalis on the first of the five days of the holiday. It was also considered to be Minerva's birthday, and no blood could be spilled or swords drawn on that day. The following four days included games and other rites in her honor. In the first century CE, the emperor Domitian established a body of priests whose duty it was to perform plays and poetry and to arrange games and circuses, all for the Quinquatria. She had two other festivals throughout the year, but Quinquatria is her main holiday.

The feast of the Quinquatria was particularly important to artists and craftsmen because Minerva was their special patron. Called the Goddess of a Thousand Crafts, the following paid special attention to Minerva, lest their trade suffer: weavers, laundresses, dyers or felt-makers, shoemakers, doctors, teachers, stonecutters, painters and sculptors.

Minerva came to Rome as the Etruscan Goddess Menrva, who was associated with measurement and numbers. She also may have replaced an earlier Latin Goddess called Nerio who had connections to Mars. Beginning in the second century BCE, Minerva was linked to the Greek Athena, that fierce, wise Goddess who sprang fully formed from the head of her father, clanging her weapons and howling for war. In contrast, while the Romans did recognize her as a martial Goddess, she was never considered as warlike in Rome as she was in Greece. She was also worshipped in Rome under the titles Minerva Medica—patron of doctors—and Minerva Capta—Minerva in Captivity—in remembrance of one of her statues being seized from a nearby town during a raid in Rome's earliest days. Through her healing association, she later became associated with baths in Roman Britain because those bodies of water were also considered to have healing powers.

Cicero relates some of the various forms of the Goddess and her widespread worship:

First is the Minerva whom we said is the mother of Apollo. Second is the one born from the Nile, whom the Egyptians of Sais worship. The third is she who we said was fathered by Jove and the fourth is the daughter of Jove and Oceanus' daughter Coryphe, whom the Arcadians call the Maiden and whom they say was the inventor of the four-horse chariot. The fifth is Pallas, who is said to have killed her father for trying to violate her virginity and whom they say has winged ankles.

–Cicero, *de Natura Deorum,*
tr. Mab Borden

Antique engraving of Minerva enthroned.

Tubilustrium

On the last day of Quinquatria, Romans gathered in the Atrium Sutorium—the Hall of the Shoemakers—to purify and bless the trumpets. This was a *lustratio*—a rite of cleansing that averted evil and brought good luck. The trumpets would be gathered in the center of the hall, and purificatory items were carried in a circle around them three times with dancing, singing and other music. These cleansing items could be torches, other instruments or animals about to be sacrificed, and the people who were chosen to carry them were selected because their names were considered particularly lucky. The circumambulation was followed by the sacrifice of a lamb to Mars, and later to Minerva as well. The *haruspices*—priests who interpreted signs—would scrutinize the entrails of the sacrificed animals for portents. A haruspex would stand with his right foot on the ground and his left on a stone, and holding the liver in his left hand, read whatever signs were exhibited upon it in a clockwise manner.

This particular lustratio is an example of a standard kind of ritual cleansing that freed an object, place or person from the influence of hostile or unlucky spirits. The elements found in all are the repeated circumambulation and the sacrifice. Trumpets themselves were frequently used in these rites, so the Tubilustrium may be a cleansing of the very instruments of purification. A lustratio was held any time there was a new beginning. For example, babies underwent lustrations as part of the rituals of child blessing, as did armies before battle or any time they received a new commander or were joined with another army. Fields, towns and the city of Rome itself were periodically purified in this way, as was the entire Roman populace in a lustratio of the people held by the censors every five years.

Etruscan image of Calchas examining the liver
of a sacrificial animal

Aprilis
April, a hollow month

The name of this month might refer to the opening of flowers or it might derive from Apru, the Estruscan Goddess who was very much like Aphrodite. Indeed, Venus has two festivals this month and the fields are green and growing. The two oldest festivals of the month are the Fordicidia and the Robigalia, which both involve imploring the Gods to protect the crops as they grow. Together with the Parilia—a purification of the herds—they seek to ensure the bounty of the fields and the flocks.

The month began with the Veneralia—the games of Venus—on the Kalends. Both Julius Caesar and his great-nephew and adopted son Augustus traced their descent from Venus as the mother of Aeneas. Their statues and other public imagery often included dolphins, seashells, cupids and other imagery associated with the Goddess as a reminder of their ancestry. This particular festival was in honor of Venus Verticordia, Venus Who Turns Hearts.

In 114 BCE, three Vestal Virgins were found to be unchaste. One Vestal betraying her vows was a problem but three was a crisis and so the Romans turned to the Sibylline books for advice. The books instructed the Romans to construct a temple to Venus Verticordia as an act of atonement, and so they did. The dies natalis of that temple was the Kalends of April, and over time the day became a general festival in honor of that Goddess. Fortuna Virilis (virile fortune) was also honored at the start of the month—women would go to the public baths and wash themselves, clad only in myrtle wreaths. Whether this was connected with the worship of Venus Verticordia is unclear.

The Megalesia or Ludi Megalenses was a festival in honor of Cybele, who was called Magna Mater—the Great Mother—in Rome. This began as a dies natalis for her temple, and there are several other temple anniversaries this month. The temple of Fortuna Publica—the luck of the people as a whole rather than the luck of the individual—celebrated its birthday on the Nones and the Temple of Jupiter the Victor had its anniversary on the Ides. The city of Rome itself celebrated its birthday on the 21st.

The multi-day Cerealia festival began on the twelfth and held particular appeal for the plebeians. It likely originated as a rural affair but it was quite old and some of its rites were obscure even to those who practiced them. In one festival event, the people gathered in the Circus Maximus at night, where foxes with lit torches tied to their tails were released. This could have been a cleansing of the crops like at the Ambarvalia, a blessing of the harvest or simply a cruel game.

One legend tells that a boy set fire to a fox that was stealing his farm's chickens, but the creature escaped and ran through the fields, setting them ablaze. Because the crops were sacred to the grain Goddess Ceres, the fox who destroyed them was punished each year. Other events of the Cerealia included horse races, theatrical performances, banquets for the plebeians and distributions of free grain. There was also a torch race of young women wearing white to represent Proserpina, the lost daughter of the Goddess in the borrowed Greek stories.

At the Vinalia on the 23rd, the wine casks from the previous autumn's pressing were opened. Originally a libation was offered to Jupiter, but eventually it was given to both Venus and Jupiter. A temple of Venus Erycina was built in the second century BCE. This form of the Goddess came from Eryx in Sicily and was considered more appropriate for the lower classes. Prostitutes would bring her offerings of mint, myrtle and rose-covered reeds on the day of the Vinalia.

Two days after the Vinalia, the Romans sacrificed to Robigus, the divine spirit of the dreaded rust blight. The Robigalia was an ancient celebration of pure propitiation, ritual appeasement of a menacing natural force. The population had reason to dread the red mildew, a scourge sometimes attacking grain—the city's principal food—and causing widespread famine. For the holiday, people dressed in white and flocked to the grove of Robigus, about five miles from Rome amid the farmland where the flamen Quirinalis let the rites. The ceremony included the sacrifice of sheep and dogs and the consultation of their innards for auguries.

The month ended with the plebeian revel of the Floralia and the ancient Latin Festival that was both a renewal of a political alliance and a celebration of shared Latin cultural identity. Take note of the following dates:

1st of the month: the Kalends of Aprilis

1st of the month: Veneralia

1st of the month: rites of Fortuna Virilis

4th–10th of the month: Ludi Megalenses

5th of the month: the Nones of Aprilis

5th of the month: dies natalis of the temple of Fortuna Publica

12th–19th of the month: Cerealia

13th of the month: the Ides of Aprilis

13th of the month: dies natalis of the Temple of Jupiter Victor

15th of the month: Fordicidia

21st of the month: dies natalis of Rome

21st of the month: Parilia

23rd of the month: Vinalia

25th of the month: Robigalia

27th of the month: Floralia

Moveable feast this month: Feriae Latinae

Ludi Megalenses

In Phrygia, the divine Agdistis was born both male and female. The Gods castrated Agdistis and she became a solely female Goddess. Where the deity's male organs touched the ground, a sweet-blossomed almond tree arose from the soil. The river God Sangarius whose waters flow through Anatolia had a daughter named Nana. One day the girl passed by the tree and plucked one of the fragrant blooms. By doing so, she conceived the child Attis. When the boy became a man, Agditis loved him passionately and desired no other, but he wished to marry someone else. In her jealous rage, the Goddess drove him mad and he castrated himself beneath a pine tree, bleeding to death there.

Agdistis was also called Cybele and given the title of Magna Mater—the Great Mother—in Rome. Cybele was the mother of all living things—vegetation, animals, humans and the Gods themselves. She might cure disease or she might inflict it. She personified sexuality and fertility, the entire process of birth, growth and death. This Goddess is sometimes sublime, sometimes savage. She is as strange as her realm—life itself. Fertile and wild, she was attended by lions who flanked the throne where she sat in her mural crown, holding the drum and libation bowl on her lap. The cult of Cybele was known for seeking to induce frenzied, ecstatic states which resulted in prophecy and immunity to pain.

There are other versions of the story of Cybele and Attis, some involving Zeus or Dionysus or Midas, but all versions agree that there was a jealous argument and that Attis castrated himself and died. In some stories he also returns to life. In a parallel to myths of Persephone, Attis was associated with vegetation and the promise of renewed life after death. A pine tree was carried through the streets for him at cult

festivals, and the societies of tree carriers also acted as burial societies. There were priestesses involved in the cult and also two types of priests of Attis. These were the Corybantes priests who were also connected to other orgiastic cults, and the Galli, priests named after the Gallus River in Turkey near the original cult center of Cybele. They used the rooster—a *gallus*—as their symbol. The Galli castrated themselves in imitation of Attis with potsherds and other crude weapons and in the rites of the Goddess, they drew blood through self-flagellation.

During the Punic Wars, the Carthaginians were threatening Italy and Rome consulted both the Sibylline books and the oracle at Delphi. A prophecy was revealed that informed the Romans that if they brought Cybele to Italy, they would be able to drive out the Carthaginians. They sought out Magna Mater's cult center at Pessinus in Phrygia (modern central Turkey) and brought a sacred black stone from there to Rome. Having no temple for this foreign Goddess, they originally placed the stone in the temple of Victoria for thirteen years until they completed the construction of a temple for Cybele, which was dedicated in 191 BCE. The Megalesia games honored the dies natalis of this temple. She eventually had several other temples and shrines as well.

During the weeklong Megalesia—which may have begun in March rather than April—a statue of the Goddess was carried through the city by her priests, accompanied by the pine tree of Attis, while the long haired, perfumed Galli covered in blood flagellated themselves. This parade wound its way through the streets to the sound of drums, tambourines, cymbals, howling songs and the curved Berecyntian flute, recalling the journey of the black stone to the Palatine when the Goddess first entered the city. The festival also included plays and games in the Circus Maximus, with the greatest games on the tenth in honor of Cybele's birthday. In early times, the games were almost the whole celebration, but plays, sacrifices and feasts were added over time. Each day had specific rites.

THE PINE TREE RITUAL, AWAKENING OF ATTIS

On the first day, a pine tree symbolic of Attis was carried to the Temple of Cybele with great ceremony. The trunk was swathed in white wool like a corpse and decked with violets. On the second day the chief ceremony was a blowing of trumpets to awaken the dead Attis.

THE DAY OF BLOOD, EVENING RESURRECTION

There followed the ominous Day of Blood. The high priest drew blood from his arms and spattered it around the altar as an offering.

The novices, wrought to the highest pitch of religious frenzy, sacrificed their virility and dashed the severed portions against the image of the implacable goddess. These broken instruments of fertility were reverently wrapped and buried, considered instrumental in recalling Attis to life and hastening the general resurrection of nature, then bursting into leaf and blossom in the spring sunshine. At nightfall mourning turned to joy: Attis had risen. The priest touched the lips of the mourners with balm and whispered into their ears glad tidings of salvation. The resurrection of the God was hailed, promising disciples their own triumph over the grave.

THE DAY OF JOY

The following day was called the Hilaria, the Day of Joy. It was a licentious carnival, with orgiasts masked and costumed. The day after was unsurprisingly a day of rest.

FESTIVE PROCESSION OF STATUE, CHARIOT RACES

The festival concluded with a magnificent procession—a silver statue of Cybele drawn in a wagon by garlanded oxen. Cybele's orchestra of flutes, drums, cymbals and horns attended and the procession wound its way to a tributary of the Tiber, the Almo. There the purple-robed high priest washed the Statue and on its return the idol was pelted with fresh spring flowers. Chariot races followed and all was gaiety.

From other areas of the Hellenistic world come tales of ritual meals, bull sacrifices and rites held in underground chambers. The Romans, however, had a complex relationship with Magna Mater. Hers was always considered a foreign and somewhat savage cult but it was sanctioned by the Sibylline books and the state had explicit obligations to it. Roman citizens could not become priests because of the castration requirement. This restriction was removed by the emperor Claudius in the first century CE, and the cult of Cybele became a prominent mystery cult in the early empire, with worship of Cybele spreading to the provinces. It survived at least until the 4th century CE and may have influenced Christian Gnosticism.

Livy describes Magna Mater's entrance to the city in the form of the black stone.

With the whole body of citizens spread out along the way, the Goddess made her way in in through their hands, passed from one to the other. They placed censors before the doors she went by, praying as the incense burned that she might enter the city of Rome willingly and be favorably inclined to them. They carried the Goddess to the temple of Victory which is on the Palatine on the day before the Ides of April, and that day was a holiday. The people crowded into the Palatine with gifts for the Goddess and they held a banquet for the Gods with couches for them to recline on, and the games called Megalesia.

–Livy, *ab Urbe Condita,*
tr. Mab Borden

The Fordicidia

This festival was said to go back to the time of Rome's great establisher of religion, its second king Numa Pompilius. A year came when there was not enough rain, and then too much, when calves were born prematurely and sheep were dying in childbirth. Numa visited a sacred grove that had a reputation for answering questions in its silence. Numa killed two sheep—one for Faunus and one for Sleep—and spread out the fleeces on the ground. He washed his head with spring water twice and donned two garlands of beech leaves. Rather than using a traditional formula, Numa offered prayers from the heart and then lay down on the sacrificial fleeces to sleep. When dark fell, the Rustic God came to him and gave him a riddle—he told Numa to placate Tellus by sacrificing two lives in the slaughter of a single heifer. Numa pondered the meaning of the dream but was unable to solve it until talking over it with his wife. A devotee of Diana, she knew its meaning and so on the fifteenth of this month every year thereafter, thirty-one pregnant cows were sacrificed to Tellus Mater, Mother Earth. One of the oldest Goddesses worshiped from the early days of Rome, she called upon to ensure the fertility of the fields and the bounty of the harvest. Typically shown in repose, Tellus' lush figure lounged on the ground, surrounded by fruit, flowers and a cornucopia.

This holiday falls within the Cerealia, a festival of Ceres, with whom Tellus is closely associated. Of the sacrifices, one of the heifers was offered on the Capitol and one in each of the thirty curae. These *holocaust* offerings—ones in which the entire animal was burned for the Gods, rather than the more typical method of the people sharing in the God's meal by consuming the edible portions of the animal and only burning the inedible parts. Vestal Virgins would attend the Fordicidia and remove the unborn calf from the womb of its mother, burn it separately and use its ashes later in the month at the Parilia.

Parilia

On the 21st—the same day as the birthday of Rome—the Romans held a purification rite to cleanse both sheep and shepherds. In this ritual they appealed to Pales, a God whose gender is uncertain, and who could have been male or female as the early Romans were frequently vague about the gender of the Gods. Pales could even be a shared name of a double deity with male and female forms, such as Liber and Libera. Pales is a name that could be either masculine or feminine and little other than the name survives. Whatever gender he or she was, Pales was a shepherd and protector of both herders and flocks and there were distinct rites in the countryside and in the city.

In the rural form of the festival, sheep pens were decorated with green branches and garlands hung on the gates. As soon as the first light began to turn the sky grey before the dawn, shepherds would begin to cleanse the enclosures. First they sprinkled them with water and swept them out, then touched the sheep with burning sulphur to make them bleat. They made bonfires of pine, male olive branches, laurel and herbs. The crackling of the flames was considered lucky. Shepherds would offer cakes, grain and milk to Pales. Then facing East, shepherds said a specific prayer four times and washed their hands in living water. This was followed by consuming a drink made of boiled wine mixed with milk and then jumping the fire three times.

In the city, most of the country rites were carried out by a priest, but there were additions as well. On the Palatine, the Vestals would blend the ashes from the unborn calf sacrificed at the Fordicidia with blood from the October Horse and sprinkle the mixture on a fire made of bean stalks. The people who attended the festival would leap three times through these flames and be sprinkled by bay leaves dipped in water.

Vestal

Julius Caesar added games to the Parilia and throughout the imperial period various ceremonies and entertainments were added to the festival. In the second century CE, it was altered by Hadrian to focus primarily on the birthday of Rome.

Shepherd's Prayer to Pales

Look after both the sheep and the shepherd.
May anything that might do harm be driven
out and flee from my stalls.
Whether I have fed the sheep in a sacred place

or if I sat under a sacred tree,
unaware that the sheep were grazing on a grave,
or if I have entered a forbidden wood or
the nymphs and the half-goat God fled at the
sight of me,
if my sickle stripped a sacred grove of its
shady bough
for canes to give to a sick sheep,
pardon my guilt!
And don't hold it against me that during the
hail storm
I brought the flock under the cover of a
country shrine.
Do not harm me for disturbing the pool.
Pardon me, nymphs,
if restless hooves stirred up the dark waters.
Goddess, appease the springs and the divine
spirits of the springs for me,
and also the Gods who are scattered
throughout each forest.
Let me not catch sight of the dryads or Diana
at her bath,
or Faunus when he lays down in the fields in
the middle of the day.
Drive sickness far away—let men and herds
be healthy
and let the watchful pack of guarding dogs be
healthy
and may I not drive back less than the
multitude of sheep that were there in
the morning

and may I not sigh, bringing back the fleeces
snatched from the wolf.
May cruel famine stay away. Let there be
plenty of grass and foliage
and washing water and drinking water.
May I press full udders and may the cheese
bring money to me,
may the thin twigs strain out the flowing whey.
And let the ram be lustful and the one he joins
with become pregnant
and may there be many lambs in my stable.
And may the wool that comes from them be
soft and bring injury to no girls,
and let it prove suitable no matter what for
delicate hands.
Let these things I pray for come about,
and we will make enormous cakes every year
for Pales, mistress of the shepherds."

—Ovid, *Fasti*, tr. Mab Borden

Floralia

On April 28, 238 BCE there was a severe drought in Rome. The afflicted Romans consulted the Sibylline Books, which recommended the dedication of a temple and games. For this reason, the Romans dedicated a temple to Flora, Goddess of the blooms, regeneration and the pleasures of youth, although she already had a cult in the city. Flora most likely originated as a Sabine Goddess and came into Rome in its early days. The temple was placed near a temple of Ceres and there may have been some connection between the two Goddesses. The rites were led by the flamen Florialis and involved sacrifices that took place in a sacred grove. The festival overall was not characterized by stately, dignified ceremonies, though. A festival of the people, Floralia was a day when drunkenness prevailed and the poet Ovid assures us that "indecency was let loose." Citizens wore colorful clothing, there were licentious theater performances with nude actors and the Circus Maximus provided the mass frenzy of chariot races. The prostitutes of Rome embraced the goddess in her sexual aspect as their own deity and observed the Floralia as their own holiday. Medals with obscene images were flung to the populace, as well as lupines, beans and vetches. Hares and goats—ancient symbols of proliferation—were released, their chase amid the legs of the crowd inspiring uproarious laughter. Throughout all, joy reigned supreme.

The Romans must have enjoyed the holiday as in later periods they kept the carousal going until May 3rd and the time span included the woman's festival of Maia on May 1st. The Floralia was probably far older than the founding of the temple, considering the nature of the Goddess and the character of the seasonal rites, invoking both the fertility of the Earth and that of mankind.

Feriae Latinae

An ancient festival enduring for more than a thousand years, the Feriae Latinae—the Latin Festival—was older than Rome itself. An annual renewal of the alliance of cities called the Latin League, it was originally dominated by Alba Longa, and by Rome only after it had taken control of the region. Despite the proliferation of petty wars between Latin states, the Latin League was a treaty of mutual defense against other peoples and powers in the region, particularly the Etruscans. The festival itself, though, may be even older than the league or the formation of city-states in the region. The Latins were a group of people with a shared culture living in central Italy from the Bronze Age on. They shared a language and religion and also had similar social structures, institutions and mutually held political rights, such as the right to marry or do business with a citizen of another Latin city, or to emigrate to a different Latin city. Citizens of other members of the Latin League were granted Roman citizenship in the fourth century BCE and the league was dissolved. The festival, however, continued because it was not just a celebration of political alliance but an affirmation of a tribal identity in which Rome shared.

The Feriae Latinae was always celebrated in April, and the consuls fixed the date for each year. This holiday in honor of Jupiter Latiares—Jupiter of the Latins—convened magistrates from every Latin town gathering annually on the Alban Mount about thirteen miles Southeast of Rome. At the festival site stood a temple dedicated to Jupiter where the main ritual took place. There were also two days of games and the people hung oscilla—small dolls and masks—in the trees. The event was considered so important that attendance was compulsory for the Latin magistrates or their deputies.

At the temple, the Roman consul offered a libation of milk, while the magistrates offered sheep, cheeses or the like. But the essential rite was the slaughter of a pure white heifer that had never felt the yoke. Then the flesh of the victim was divided among the groups in attendance and eaten. To miss the sacramental meal would denote loss of communion with Jupiter and the Latin league and celebrants made certain to appear and obtain their allotted flesh. The least oversight signified an evil omen, and the sacrifice would then need to be repeated, which sometimes happened. Each year the festival affirmed a kinship of blood, sealed by sharing a common meal of a sacrificial animal—in such a way entering into solemn communion with Jupiter, the victim and each other.

Jupiter

Maius
May, a full month

The name of this month possibly derives from Maia, a Goddess with no cult but who is the mother of Mercury in mythology, or from *maior*, the Latin word for greater, perhaps referring to the growth of the crops and anticipation of the harvest. The explanation most closely tied to the festivities of the month, though, is that the name could come from *maiores*—the ancestors—who are propitiated on three days this month for the Lemuria holiday.

The month begins with the priests setting up an altar with images of the Lares Praestites—the guardian spirits of the city of Rome rather than the Lares of the household. The city, though, necessarily had all the religious attributes of a home—a hearth in the form of the Vestal flame, an entrance presided over by Janus and Lares to guard it. Ovid mentions a statue of a dog being set out with the Lares Praestites to indicate their watchful loyalty to those who dwell within their domain.

Also on the first of the month is the anniversary of the temple of Bona Dea. Her name simply means, "the Good Goddess" and she was associated with Faunus as either his wife or his sister. Her cult was exclusive to women and her primary festival—which was held in the home of a high-ranking magistrate rather than in the temple—was in December. While that rite was primarily attended by women from the patrician class, her May festival was celebrated by the plebeians. The temple itself was a center for healing and was frequented by snakes like the temple of Aesculapius. Neither men nor myrtle were allowed inside. Her preferred sacrifice was a sow.

The April festival of Flora which began in April came to its conclusion on the third, and then the Nones passed before the curiously separated holiday of the Lemuria begins. These rites of the dead took place on the ninth, eleventh and thirteenth but not on the tenth or twelfth and they were private rituals in the home rather than state-run sacrifices. The Argei made their first procession around the city in March. On the fourteenth of this month, these straw dolls or effigies were bound hand and foot and once again paraded through the city before being cast into the Tiber. At the May procession, however, the Flaminica Dialis—the wife of the high priest of Jupiter—attended in mourning garb. On the same day, the temple of Mars Invictus (Unconquered) had its anniversary.

Jove and Mercury both have feasts on the Ides. The third of the four Agonalia of the year—the others are in February, March and December—occurs six days later and was marked by a ram sacrifice by the rex sacrorum. A festival for Vediovis—an inverse form of Jove—was also held on the 21st and a second purification of the trumpets on the twenty-third. The main festival of the fire God Vulcan was in August, but there was also a smaller festival for him on May twenty-third.

On the twenty-fifth is the dies natalis of the temple of Fortuna Primigenia—the Fortune of the Firstborn. There is one moveable festival this month, Ambarvalia which is related to the Amburbium in February. It was usually celebrated at the end of the month, with the twenty-ninth as an approximate date. Take note of the following dates:

1st of the month: the Kalends of Maius

1st of the month: day of the Lares Praestites

1st of the month: dies natalis of the temple of Bona Dea

3rd of the month: celebration for Flora

7th of the month: the Nones of Maius

9th, 11th and 13th of the month: Lemuria

14th of the month: procession of the Argei

14th of the month: dies natalis of the temple of Mars Invictus

15th of the month: the Ides of Maius, the beginning of summer

15th of the month: Feriae of Jove

15th of the month: Mercuralia

21st of the month: Agonalia

21st of the month: festival of Vediovis

23rd of the month: Feriae of Vulcan

23rd of the month: Tubilustrium

25th of the month: dies natalis of the temple of Fortuna Primigenia

Moveable feast this month: Ambarvalia

Lemuria

The legend goes that after Romulus laid his slain twin's ashes and bones to rest in his tomb, his foster parents returned to their home. As they sat slumped on the couch, worn out with grief, Remus appeared before them, still covered in blood. His ghostly voice was faint as he lamented, regretting his death and his failure to become ruler of the new city. He compared Romulus to a wolf, recalling the gentleness of the wolf who suckled them as children and also remembering his brother's swift violence. He then blamed rashness itself for his death, saying that Romulus was a devoted brother who grieved Remus' cruel fate and he told them to entreat Romulus— who was now king—to set aside a day for him. The shepherd and his wife reached out for the child they'd raised for so long, but the shade slipped away from their grasping fingers. The king agreed to their request, and so the holiday was placed in the calendar. In those early days it was called Remuria after Remus but over time the sound softened and the name became Lemuria.

Ovid claims to have heard this tale of the origin of the holiday from Mercury himself, but the origin of the ancient rite and the reasons for the alternating days—the ninth, eleventh and thirteenth—are unknown. On these days, temples were closed and there could be no weddings. For the entire month weddings were generally considered unlucky but were forbidden on the days of the Lemuria.

The Romans practiced both cremation and inhumation and elaborate tombs lined the roads outside the city. On the days of the Lemuria, the people visited the graves of their ancestors and made offerings to them. There was also a nocturnal rite performed

Roman Sarcophagi at the Side Archaeological Museum in Turkey

by the *pater familias*—the oldest male member or patriarch of the family. It would take place before the ancestral shrine in the home, where veneration of the *maiores*—deceased ancestors—took place throughout the year.

Their physical remains might rest outside the city walls, but the Romans kept the death masks of their ancestors in the home. These were made of beeswax and kept in a niche in the atrium of the house. When there was a funeral, living members of the family would wear the ancestors' masks for the procession along with clothes appropriate to the offices and honors each ancestor held. The masks themselves were made during a person's life rather than after death, usually upon gaining a particularly high political office or attaining some notable achievement. Having your mask made signaled that you were becoming worthy of your ancestors. This ancestral shrine in the home also held lists of the offices held by ancestors, a genealogy and armor and weapons seized during significant military campaigns. The whole served as a display of the prominence of the family as well as a place of veneration where the masks became stained with incense smoke over the generations. Because wax is not a durable material, wealthier families might replace a wax mask with a stone sculpture of the head and shoulders—a bust. The practice of making a bust of a prominent person comes down to modern times but has lost its funerary connotations.

During the Lemuria, the father of the family would rise in the silence of midnight. Without shoes, he made the *manu fico* to ward against ghosts. This sign is a closed fist with the thumb between the fingers and is still used in Italy and elsewhere to ward off evil. Approaching the faces of his venerated fathers, the man washed his hands with spring water and took a handful of black beans in his fist. He turned all the way around and then turned his face away to throw the beans, saying nine times, "These I cast. With these beans I atone for me and mine!" He kept his face turned away the entire time and after the prayer, he washed again. Then he clashed bronze cymbals together to drive out the ghosts and yelled nine times, "ancestral shades, get out!"

Mercuralia

On the Ides of May, Romans might try in vain to purchase much of anything, for on this day tradesmen shut up shop and gathered at the temple of Mercury. They were paying tribute to the God of commerce and the market, the son of Maia and Jupiter. The Roman counterpart of the Greek Hermes, of all the deities he was the trickiest and most glib. This fraud-loving god, generally depicted with a bulging purse, could sell you the Colosseum. His symbols included those seen in Greece—the caduceus, cap of invisibility and winged sandals—as well as the ram, goat, rooster and turtle. Mercury was also one of the most commonly worshipped of the Roman Gods in the provinces and was frequently syncretized with a number of Celtic, Germanic and Iberian Gods by the Romanized peoples in those regions.

The festival of Mercury was celebrated annually on the anniversary of the dedication of the temple of Mercury in 495 BCE following a great famine. The cult's founding merchants assumed that a bit of smart trading would prevent starvation and promote prosperity—with a little help from a friend with divine clout. The temple with its plebeian roots was modest, its annual celebration serving as both religious tribute and expression of guild solidarity, especially by grain merchants. Patricians looked down on the cult but that didn't seem to slow down its popularity. Altars, statues, murals and small-roofed shrines to Mercury dotted busy urban intersections throughout Rome.

The only temple of Mercury in Rome, though, was on the Aventine and this served as a center for the trade guilds. There is a legend of a spring dedicated to the God near one of the gates of Rome. There, merchants washed their hands, tucked up their tunics and waded in to take some of the water. They used laurel leaves to sprinkle both themselves and their wares with this sacred water, praying to Mercury to wash away any lies they've told for the sake of trade. Then they'd add a prayer that the Gods not be upset when they lie in the future and ask for profit, joy from profit and pleasure from deceiving their buyers. This brings a laugh to Mercury's lips because he himself stole Apollo's cattle.

Horace Ode 1.10 to Mercury
Mercury, eloquent grandson of Atlas,
clever one who shaped the uncivilized customs of
inexperienced humanity
by your voice and by the manners
of the honorable wrestling school.
I will sing of you, herald of mighty Jove and of the Gods,
creator of the curved lyre,
whom it pleases to conceal every crafty thing
with tricks and jokes.
Once Apollo tried to intimidate you when you were a boy,
demanding that you give back the cows you'd stolen for a trick.
Then he noticed that his quiver, too,
had vanished while he was using his threatening voice,
and he laughed.
Not only that, but with you leading him, wealthy Priam
deceived the haughty descendant of Atreus
and the Thessalonian watchfires and the camps hostile to Troy,
when he had left Ilium behind.
You restore pious souls to happy seats
and you hold back the feather-light multitude with your
golden wand,
you who are welcome in the high places of the gods
and in the depths.

—tr. Mab Borden

Ambarvalia

At this moveable festival, the Romans drove animals along the boundaries of fields and sacrificed at various points along the route. They beat the ground as they went to drive off any baneful influences. The Ambarvalia was celebrated as both a public and private rite—farmers did no work and the day was given over to celebration. This purification of the crops also involved a larger procession around the fields which demarcated Roman territory. Both the beating on the ground and the purpose to bless the fields point to the chthonic Gods of agriculture, namely Ceres, protector of the grain.

Ceres was closely associated with the Greek Demeter. She had several temples in Rome that could serve as grain distribution centers for the poor, making her popular with urban plebeians as well as with farmers. She received sacrifices after funerals to purify a house from the taint of death. The practice of walking the fields to purify them at the beginning of the agricultural cycle survives in Christian Rogation Day rituals.

Georgics 1.335-350
Keep watch of the months and the stars
of the sky,
notice where Saturn's cold planet
receives himself,
and into what kind of orbit in heaven the fire
of Mercury might wander.
Most importantly, venerate the Gods and offer
back the annual rites

to great Ceres—render sacrifice on the grass
which is happy
that the last part of winter is finally defeated
now that it is the bright spring.
This is the time when lambs are fat, this is
when wine is most mellow,
when sleep is sweet and shadows are dense
on the mountains.
Let your whole population of the countryside
honor Ceres,
bathe the honeycomb in milk and mild
wine for her,
let the blessed sacrificial victim march three
times around the new crops,
with the whole chorus of companions
following with rejoicing
and they call Ceres indoors with a shout,
and do not let anyone put the sickle to the ripe
ears of grain

                                        —Virgil, tr. Mab Borden

Junius
June, a hollow month

Ovid depicts three Goddesses giving different possible origins for the name of the month, with each claiming it was named in her honor. Juno's argument is simplest and likeliest, but Juventas (Youth) says it is similarly derived from her name. Because the name of the Goddess Juno also possibly derives from the word for youth, there is no settling this argument. The last claimant is Concordia (Harmony,) who says that the name of the month comes from the word *iungo* (join) in honor of Concordia's joining the Sabines with the Romans in the early days of the city.

The month opens with a festival of Cardea, the Goddess of hinges, on the Kalends. This day is also the anniversary of the temple Mars on the slope outside the Porta Capena and of the temple of Juno Moneta—who looked after the financial welfare of the city—and because "Moneta" is similar to *monere* (to warn,) there was a tradition that this form of Juno was also the one who used her sacred geese to warn the Romans of the approach of the attacking Gallic army in 390 BCE. The temple was vowed to the Goddess by the general Camillus in 345 BCE during a different war with the Aurunci in Southern Italy.

Another temple outside the Porta Capena—the temple of the Tempestates—also celebrated its birthday on the Kalends, and like the temple of Juno Moneta, was constructed in fulfillment of a vow. During the first Punic War with Carthage, the general Lucius Cornelius Scipio was leading his fleet near Corsica when a storm began to ravage the sea. He begged the Tempestates—Goddesses of the Storm—to deliver them and vowed the temple if his prayer were fulfilled.

Two days later the temple of Bellona has its anniversary. Situated just outside the walls near the altar of Mars, the senate would receive returning generals here, where they would lay down their command before re-entering the city. Bellona was an ancient Goddess who ruled over warfare. Originally called Duellona, she was associated with Mars as either sister or wife, and she was identified with a number of other Goddesses, including the Greek Enyo, the early Italian Nerio and Ma the mother Goddess of Cappadocia, where she was called Ma-Bellona. As Nerio, the personification of valor, she received the spoils of war. A short column called the Column of War stood outside her temple. When the senate declared war on an enemy, the *fetialis*—a priest who oversaw treaties and other foreign affairs—would throw a spear over the column to represent an attack on enemy territory.

Two temples of Hercules have anniversaries this month, the temple of Hercules Custos on the fourth and Hercules Musarum on the twenty-ninth. Dius Fidius is honored on the Nones. This God of oaths was identified with both Hercules and Jupiter, and when Romans took oaths, they went out into the open air and said, "*me Hercule* (by Hercules,)" "*me*

Dius Fidius" (by Dius Fidius,) or less commonly but with much more solemnity, *"per Iovem"* (through Jove.)

Two days after the Nones are the Ludi Piscatorii—the Fishermen's games. All fish caught at this festival for the God of the Tiber River were sacrificed by fire at the temple of Vulcan. On the same day, the festival of Vesta begins, which includes a *dies religiosus* on the 9th and continues through the fifteenth. Overlapping with that festival are several more temple anniversaries, the Matralia and the Feriae of Jove on the Ides. The temple of Mens Bona (the Good Mind) honored the personified ideal of rightmindedness.

The Matralia was a festival honoring mothers on the eleventh. Held in honor of the ancient Goddess Mater Matuta, a Goddess associated with children, child rearing and the dawn. The strange rites of this involved decorating the cult statue, beating a slave girl in the temple and baking sacrificial cakes in old-fashioned clay vessels and offering them to Mater Matuta. Women prayed first for their nieces and nephews, and then for their own children. The temple of this Goddess was just inside the Porta Carmentalis and dates to the sixth century BCE, from the period of the monarchy. Known for its brightly colored terracotta decorations, the temple burned down and was rebuilt several times. Even when it was rebuilt, it had an archaic style altar in the shape of a U. The inner chamber of this temple was incorporated into the church of Sant'Omobono.

Fortuna is honored twice this month, with temple anniversaries on the eleventh and festival on the twenty-fourth. A lesser Quinquatria festival than the one in March was held for Minerva on the thirteenth through fifteenth and she was also honored on the ninteenth at the commemoration of the temple of Minerva on the Aventine—the anniversary was mainly celebrated in March. On the twentieth, Summanus the God of nocturnal thunder was honored, one of nine Thunder Gods. The Lares were honored on the twenty-seventh, the same day as the dedication of the temple of Jupiter Stator, Jupiter the Stayer. This form of the God caused soldiers to stand their ground in battle rather than flee before an enemy. Jupiter Stator had two temples in Rome. The temple with its anniversary on this day was built in fulfillment of a vow made by Marcus Atilius Regulus in 294 BCE, when the Roman army rallied in a battle against the Samnites, an Italic people living in Southern Italy.

The end of the month celebrates the temple of Hercules Musarum, Hercules of the Muses, sometimes also called the temple of Hercules and the Muses. The Taurian Games for the *di inferi* (the Gods of the Underworld) are a moveable feast usually held on the twenty-fifth and twenty-sixth. Take note of the following dates:

1st of the month: the Kalends of Junius

1st of the month: festival of Cardea

1st of the month: dies natalis of the temple of Juno Moneta

1st of the month: dies natalis of the temple of Mars

1st of the month: dies natalis of the temple of the Tempestates

3rd of the month: dies natalis of the temple of Bellona

4th of the month: dies natalis of the temple of Hercules Custos

5th of the month: the Nones of Junius

5th of the month: dies natalis of the temple of Dius Fidius

7th of the month: Ludi Piscatorii, the Fishermen's Games

7th–15th of the month: Vestalia

8th of the month: dies natalis of the temple of Mens Bona

11th of the month: Matralia for Mater Matuta

11th of the month: dies natalis of the temple of Fortuna in the Forum Boarium

13th of the month: the Ides of Junius

13th–15th of the month: Quinquatrus Minisculae

19th of the month: dies natalis of the temple of Minerva on the Aventine

20th of the month: anniversary of the temple of Summanus

24th of the month: Festival of Fors Fortuna

27th of the month: honoring the Lares

27th of the month: dies natalis of the temple of Jupiter Stator

29th of the month: dies natalis of the temple of Hercules Musarum

Moveable feast this month: Taurian Games, usually held around the 25th–26th

Festival of Cardea

The tale goes that Cardea, the Goddess of Hinges, attained her power through misfortune. She was a nymph called Cranaë who haunted the grove of Alernus. She was beautiful and had many suitors but she spurned them all, preferring Diana's path. She was frequently seen hunting in the countryside, pursuing wild beasts with javelins and laying traps by spreading nets across valley floors. She was often mistaken for Diana herself, even though she carried no bow or quiver.

When she was pursued by would-be lovers, she tricked them. They would whisper their propositions to her and she would feign both interest and modesty, telling them that the open places had too much sunlight. The Sun would shine on their dalliance, bringing shame to her, but if a suitor could lead the way to a more hidden place, a close glade or grotto, she would follow. Each time, the eager young man would lead the way, and each time, Cranae would slip away and hide, unable to be found. It always worked, until the one pursuing her was Janus.

When the God of the Doorways came to her with soft, sweet words, hard-hearted Cranae whispered her usual reply. When Janus turned to lead her to a cave, she hid as she usually did, but the two-faced God saw her hiding place, seized her and raped her. To repay her for her virginity (whether as a guilt gift or by some legalistic understanding,) Janus gave Cranae dominion over hinges. He also gifted her with a long, white thorn to drive away any unwanted person from the doorway.

She used this power in particular to guard babies in their cradles. Evil spirits would take the form of owls and hunt by night for any unguarded infants, snatching them up and tearing tender flesh from tiny bones. These *striga*—who might also be Witches transformed into birds—came one night to the bedroom of five-day-old Proca. The birds began to attack him but his nursemaid heard the baby's cries and came running and chased off the striga. As the nurse began to tend the poor child's wounds, she despaired, and so she called on Cranae. The Goddess came to Proca's cradle and told the nurse and the parents to lay aside their fear because she herself would heal him.

Cranae took an arbutus branch and touched it three times to the doorposts, then three times she marked the threshold with it. She sprinkled the entryway with water that contained a *medicamen*—an herb or remedy—and then held up the bloody entrails of a two-month-old sow, intoning:

"Nocturnal birds, spare the child! In place of a small infant, receive a small victim! Take heart for heart, bowels for bowels. We give you this life as a replacement for one which is better."

Then Cranae threw the gory mess outside into the night, instructing all present to turn away and not look back. She placed the thorn of Janus below the window and afterwards the child's health was restored and the striga never approached him again.

This tale comes from Ovid, who conflates the nymph Cranae with both Carna, who guards the internal organs, and Cardea, who guards the hinge. On the Kalends of June, people ate a special meal in her honor—beans and spelt cooked in bacon fat, because Cranae was an ancient Goddess who was easily pleased with simple foods.

 Festivals of Hercules

Identified with the Greek Herakles, the Roman Hercules was a God of both victory and business ventures. Hercules had many temples, several of which were in the round rather than the typical rectangular style. Round temples were more typical in Romano-Celtic areas, but the temple of Vesta was also round. This God could receive any sacrifice at all, without preference or restriction, just as tales of the Greek hero emphasize his tendency toward indiscriminate excess in both food and drink.

Popular everywhere he went, the God was called Hercules Invictus (the Unconquered,) Hercules Victor (the Victorious,) Hercules Musarum (of the Muses,) Hercules Pompeianus and Hercules Custos (the Caretaker.) As patron of quarry workers, he was Hercules Saxanus (of the Rocks.) Hercules was identified with the Phoenician Melqart and was also extremely popular in the Celtic lands conquered by Rome, where he was identified with a number of Gallic deities under the names Hercules Magusanus, Hercules Ilunnus, Hercules Ogmios, in Britain as Hercules Saegon (Victorious.) The Cerne Abbas giant chalk figure is likely a portrait of Hercules.

In Rome itself, the round temple of Hercules Musarum contained statues of each of the Muses and of Hercules playing the lyre. Oaths were sworn at the altar of Hercules Victor and business deals could also be made there. A statue of Hercules Triumphalis (the Triumphant) was placed in the Forum Boarium along the route of the *triumph* (victory parade) that a conquering general would lead through the city. The entire army marched in the triumph, and the spoils of war were displayed for the people. Famous captives were dragged through the streets in chains—Cleopatra and Antony killed themselves after their defeat by Octavian specifically to avoid this fate. Whenever there was a parade, the statue of Hercules Triumphalis was draped with the special garb of a conquering general—the *toga palmata*, which was dyed purple and embroidered with golden palms. The expensive Tyrian purple color came from the murex snails on the Phoenician coast, and the color deepened rather than faded in the sunlight. The right to wear this toga could only come from waging and winning wars for Rome.

Hercules and Cacus

Vestalia

In the round one-room thatched huts of neolithic Italy, the hearth occupied the center. Here the family gathered for warmth and food and the same life-sustaining site served as the household altar. Before each meal the family offered scraps of food in a little bowl to Vesta, the *numen* or divine spirit of the hearth fire.

Vesta worship similarly extended into the city in a round temple that echoed the shape of a hut. Originally roofed in thatch, by the time of Augustus the roof was bronze. The spirit of Rome abided in a flame in the Forum Romanum that was kept flickering in her temple, considered the hearth of the nearby royal palace (when Rome still had kings.) The fire was tended ceremonially by six priestesses who were considered the king's daughters. They were chosen by lot between the ages of six and ten from candidates selected by the pontifex maximus for their physical perfection. Both their parents had to be living and they had to be of patrician birth. They wore elegantly distinctive clothing and a six locks hairstyle otherwise permitted only to brides. The high position of the Vestals demanded sacrifice, though—they were required to remain celibate for their thirty years of office. While most Vestals remained in service and chaste all their lives, they had the option to marry after thirty years. Lapses of purity were deemed high crimes against the state and were horrendously punished. During the long course of the cult, three priestesses lost their virginity and were buried alive.

The eternal flame was rekindled on March 1—the first day of the year in the old calendar—by the method of rubbing sticks together. Each city had a public hearth sacred to Vesta where the fire was never allowed to go out. When a new colony was founded, the colonists carried with them coals from the hearth of the mother city with which to kindle a fire on the new city's hearth. In Rome, men were forbidden from entering the temple of Vesta. Its inner room may have contained ancient statues of Penates along with other sacred items that were rescued each time the temple burned down and restored with each rebuilding. Traditionally, there were no statues of Vesta in her temples because she was represented by the flame. Augustus, however, dedicated a statue of her with an altar in his home.

At the Vestalia festival in June, the *penus* (storehouse) which served as the inner sanctuary of the temple was opened and remained open to women through the 15th. This was also a holiday of bakers and grain millers—people would hang garlands of violets on the millstones and loaves of bread around the necks of the donkeys whose labor turned them. This festival also involved a special salt cake baked by the Vestals, called a *mola salsa*, which was also used at the Epulum Jovis in September and November and the Lupercalia in February. This was made from salt, flour and water fetched from a sacred spring without setting it down on the way.

Fasti

"Now, understand that Vesta is nothing other
than living flame,
and you see no bodies born from flame.
Rightly, therefore, she is a virgin, who neither
puts out any seed nor receives any,
and she loves companions of virginity."

—Ovid, tr. Mab Borden

Summanus

The twentieth of June sees the anniversary of the temple of Summanus, one of the dii Novensiles—meaning either the new Gods or the nine Gods. They were very ancient and are likely the same as the nine Etruscan Thunder Gods. Before the founding of Rome, nine of the ancient Etruscans Gods had the specific power to hurl thunderbolts. The Etruscans also believed that there were eleven sorts of thunderbolts, although the exact differences between the bolts and the precise identities of each of the Thunder Gods is unclear. Three types of bolts were in the command of the supreme God Tinia, who was later associated with Jupiter. One kind was wielded by Cupra who was later associated with Juno and another by Sethlans who was later called Vulcan. Thunder at the Spring Equinox came from Menrva who had many shrines and was associated with both the Etruscan Goddess of fortune Nortia and with Athena. Vediovis was responsible for thunder loud enough to cause deafness, and thunder at nighttime came from Summanus. Both of these were later identified with Jupiter.

Because of the profound influence of the Etruscans on Rome, veneration of Summanus continued there, first with a statue of the God as part of the pediment sculpture adorning the temple of Jupiter Optimus Maximus. This was struck by lightning in 197 BCE, which the Romans took to mean that Summanus wanted a temple of his own. This was constructed on the west side of the Circus Maximus and was dedicated on June 20th. The God received offerings of cakes shaped like wheels and of castrated black rams. The wheel-shaped cakes were also consumed by worshippers and were not unlike hot cross buns.

Whether Summanus himself was particularly venerated in historical times is unclear. When he mentions this festival, Ovid follows the name Summanus with the phrase "whoever that is," so he was obscure by the 1st century, despite the annual maintenance of his cult. What is clear, though, is that thunder itself remained an important sign of the presence of the *numen*, a clear indicator of the attention of the divine— whatever God that might be.

Horace 1.34

While I wander, a moderate and infrequent
worshipper of the Gods,
counseled with unwise wisdom,
now I am compelled to set sail again
and to repeat the voyage I abandoned.
For Diespiter, frequently splitting the clouds with
flashing fire,
drove thundering horses and his winged chariot
through the clear sky,
until the heavy earth and the wandering rivers and
even the Styx and the grim seat of hateful
Taenarius
and the heights of Atlas all shake.
The God has the power to transform the lowest to
the highest
and to diminish the famous, lifting up the obscure.
Then grasping Fortune with shrill hissing
snatches away the crown from there,
and delights in setting it here.

–Horace, *Odes*,
tr. Mab Borden

Fortuna

Called Fors, Fortuna or Fors Fortuna—the force of Fortune, Rome had temples to the Goddess of Luck as well as a large number of shrines. Fors and Fortuna may have originated as separate Goddesses of chance and providence, but by historical times they were referred to interchangeably. She became identified with both the Greek Tyche and the Etruscan Nortia.

Particular aspects of Fortuna had their own shrines and temples. With many cult titles, it seems there was a face and an altar of Fortuna for most every situation and concern. Women appealed to Fortuna Muliebris (the Fortune of Women,) who protected their interests in particular. Upon their marriages, women would dedicate their clothing to Fortuna Virgo (Fortune the Virgin.) One of the temples of Fortuna near the temple of Mater Matuta had an archaic U-shaped altar, matching that of the archaic mother Goddess. The two temples also shared an anniversary, emphasizing the connection between the cults.

Fortuna Primigenia watched over the luck of first-born children. A sanctuary of this aspect of the Goddess in Praeneste was well-known for its oracle, who used random chance to select a response to a question from a number of pre-written answers carved into pieces of oak. Unlike at Delphi and other ancient oracles where priests interpreted the oracular responses, the meaning of the answer at Praeneste was left entirely up to the petitioner.

Shrines to Fortuna Augusta venerated the Goddess for protecting the luck of the emperor, and on the return of the emperor Augustus to Rome in 19 BCE, an altar to Fortuna Redux (Fortune Who Brings Home) was erected in the Campus Martius. This same epithet of the Goddess was honored by soldiers abroad in military bathhouses, alongside altars to Fortuna Balnearis (Fortune of the Baths) and Fortuna Salutaris (Fortuna the Bringer of Health.)

Other cult titles of Fortuna include Fortuna Conservatrix (the Preserver,) Fortuna Equestris (of the Equestrian Class,) Fortuna Mala (Bearded Fortune) and Fortuna Respiciens (Provident Fortune.) Those looking for a little undeserved luck might offer sacrifices at the shrine of Fortuna Obsequens (Indulgent Fortune) on the Caelian Hill. Fortuna Virilis (Fortune of the Virile) was venerated alongside Venus at the Veneralia on the Kalends of April, and both men and women had an interest in the gifts of this particular face of the Goddess. Fortuna Huiusque Diei (the Fortune of This Day) looked after the luck of any given day.

Two main divisions of Fortuna are Fortuna Privata and Fortuna Publica, who concern themselves with the fortune of the private individual and with the fortune of the state, respectively. Fortuna Publica had temples as Fortuna Publica Populi Romani (the Fortune of the Roman People) and Fortuna Citerior (Fortune Closer to the Center of the City.) Fortuna Romana (the Fortune of Rome) concerned herself particularly with the city of Rome itself. All could worship her—two of the earliest temples of Fors Fortuna were dedicated by *Servius* Tullius. Ovid notes that this king was the son of a slave (the family name Servius simply means "of the slave") and so it was appropriate for her worship to be open to slaves as well as free Romans.

Fortune might be petitioned and appeased, but she was also fickle and rash, and this is reflected in her varied iconography. The primary symbol of Fors Fortuna was the wheel and she was frequently depicted standing on a wheel to show the instability of Fortune. She also appears with a cornucopia to symbolize her role as provider and a rudder to symbolize her steering the destiny of humankind. She is also frequently depicted as blind, indicating the unpredictable and seemingly irrational distribution of her favors. For her June festival, worshippers would take boats across the Tiber to her temples downriver, and return the same way, drunken and garlanded.

Hymn to Fortune

O Goddess, you who rule gracious Antium,
ready either to lift up the mortal body from a low
position
or to turn proud triumphal parades into funeral
processions.
The impoverished famer in the countryside
implores you with troubled prayer.
Whoever splits the Carpathian sea with a
Bithynian keel
prays to you, mistress of the level sea.
The cruel Dacian, the Scythian exile,
all pray to you,
and the towns and the peoples and warlike Latium
and the mothers of barbarian kings
and purple-clad tyrants stand in fear of you
because you might hurl down the upright pillar
with an errant foot, or cause the turbulent crowd
to inflame the peaceable,
"To arms! To arms!" and shatter the
power of the state.
Servile Necessity always goes before you,
bearing nails for the beams,
and wedges in her bronze hand,
and the cruel dragging hooks and the molten lead

weren't left behind.
Hope cherishes you and rare Loyalty,
veiled in white, does not deny her friend
no matter how you forsake the houses
of the powerful
as a turncoat enemy.
But the faithless public and the lying harlot
fall away
and when the wine jar has been drunk down to
the lees,
deceitful friends scatter rather than bear the
yoke of hardship.

–Horace 1.35, tr. Mab Borden

Fortuna

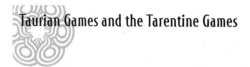 Taurian Games and the Tarentine Games

During the reign of Tarquin Superbus, the awful last king of Rome, an outbreak of plague was traced back to the sale of beef to pregnant women, whose babies were impacted as well. Games were instituted to appease the *Di Inferi*—a collective term for the Gods of the Underworld—and the plague lifted. The games themselves were held in the Circus Flaminius and included horse racing. There may have been bull sacrifice and bull leaping, fighting or other bull games. A moveable festival in June, the Taurian Games date from at least as early as the late Republic but how often they occurred is unclear—records from the second century CE indicate that the Games were held every five years under the emperor Antoninus Pius, but whether that was the case in other eras is unknown. The origin of their name is also uncertain. Ancient scholars proposed that the title could come from *taurus* (bull) or from the Etruscan *tauru* (tomb,) as they may have had an Etruscan origin and occurred on the racetrack, where the turning posts were modeled after Etruscan funeral monuments.

The Di Inferi first and foremost include Dis and Proserpina, the king and queen of the realm of the dead. The name Dis is a contraction of *dives* (rich) and is sometimes also rendered as Dis Pater, the Rich Father or the Father of Riches. He was rich in souls, as all living things flowed to his kingdom, which was located underground—where gold, silver and gems were also to be found. He may also have been associated with the richness of the soil. Dis was at times associated with Orcus, a death God who appears in Etruscan tombs as a large, hairy, bearded man and was also equated with the Greek Hades, who was called *Plouton*, a Greek word meaning "rich," with a nearly identical set of associations as Dis. Proserpina was a Latinized pronunciation of Persephone, Goddess of the Underworld and the germinating seed, in an explicit imitation of the Greek cult. The wife of Dis, she was the daughter of Ceres and the myths of Persephone were also hers in Rome. The Sabine Sun God Soranus was identified with Dis Pater as well as with Apollo, and in the northern provinces, Dis Pater was worshipped alongside a Celtic consort, the Underworld Goddess Aericura. Julius Caesar says without elaboration that the Gauls considered themselves to be descended from Dis Pater, but he only used Roman names when writing about Gallic religion, so the Celtic name of the God he was identifying with Dis Pater has been lost.

Dis and Proserpina could not be reached by ordinary prayer. Oaths and curses could be heard in their kingdom, though, and to gain their attention, worshippers would strike the ground. They would offer black sheep, turning their faces away while they performed the sacrifice, as with any interaction with the Di Inferi.

On the edge of the Campus Martius (the field of Mars) near the Tiber is the Tarentum, a small volcanic fissure that, because it once emitted vapor, was thought to be a point of contact with the underworld. A story from the early days of Rome goes that the children of the Sabine Valesius—an ancestor of the first Roman consul—had a dream in which they received instructions to dig there. Valesius set his servants to digging and they discovered a round, marble altar to Dis and Proserpina. During the first Punic War, the Sibylline Books advised instituting three nights of nocturnal games, rituals and theatrical performances at the site. These were called the Tarentine Games or the Secular Games, from *saeculum* (generation) because they were held every hundred years. The altar of Dis and Proserpina was uncovered for these Games and then covered up again for another century afterward.

While the sacrifices were somewhat different each time the games were held, an inscription from the time of Augustus lists sacrifices from that Secular Games that alternated between diurnal sacrifices to the regular Gods of Rome and nocturnal sacrifices. These were located at the altar of Dis and Proserpina in the Campus Martius but directed at other Gods of the Di Inferi who were concerned with aspects of human life—fate, birth and agriculture. For the first two days, the nocturnal offerings were in increments of nine and the diurnal in twos, and on the third day the nocturnal is in increments of two and the diurnal in nine. On the first night, nine female lambs and nine female goats were offered at the Campus Martius to the Fates. On the following day, two bulls were offered to Jupiter Optimus Maximus on the Capitoline Hill. That night at the Campus Martius, nine each of three different sacrificial cakes were given to Ilythiae, a Goddess of childbirth, and on the second day, two cows were sacrificed to Juno Regina on the Capitoline Hill. On the third night, a pregnant sow was offered to Terra Mater (Mother Earth) at the Campus Martius and on the third and last day of the festival, another twenty-seven sacrificial cakes—again in nine each of three kinds of cakes—were offered to Diana and Apollo. Each of the sacrifices was followed by dramatic performances. Augustus commissioned the poet Horace to compose a hymn—the Carmen Saeculare—for the once-in-a-lifetime event. The song addressed to Diana and Apollo was performed by three choirs of children on the Palatine and the Capitoline hills after the last sacrifice of the festival. There were then seven days of plays performed in both Greek and Latin as well as a last day of hunts and chariot racing.

Pluto abducts Proserpina

Julius
July, a full month

Originally called Quinctilis—the fifth month—in the old calendar that started in March, after Julius Caesar's assassination in 44 BCE, Mark Antony changed the name of the month to Julius in his honor because Caesar's birthday was July twelfth. The festivals this month are all fairly obscure, and they occur just as the death rate rose to its highest peak in the year. This was due to the heat, which is no small thing in the summer months in Italy and which could be quite intense in the multi-story tenements that housed the majority of the populace.

The Kalends of the month opens with a temple anniversary of Juno Felicitas—a conflation of the Goddess with the personification of good luck. On the fifth is the curious ceremony in the

Campus Martius called Poplifugia, which literally means "the flight of the people." Its meaning was unknown even in ancient times, but speculation by ancient Roman authors included that it could have commemorated the flight of the people from Rome when Fidenae—another Latin city—attacked shortly after the sack of the city by the Gauls and that it might have been held in remembrance of a rush of the people on the death of Romulus. While it is curious that the Romans might have celebrated fleeing before an enemy, they did defeat the Fidenates two days later.

The Games of Apollo began on the sixth and stretched through the thirteenth. Also on the sixth was the temple anniversary of Fortuna Muliebris—the Fortune of Women—followed by the festival of female slaves called Nonae Caprotinae or the Ancillarium Feriae on the seventh.

Two agricultural feasts were on the Nones on the seventh as well. There was a sacrifice to the Grain-God Consus, whose major festivals were in August and December. This happened at an underground altar in the Circus Maximus and the same day honored the Pales, the God of shepherds, who was also worshipped at the Parilia in April. The eighth saw the Vitulatio, a day of rest and thanksgiving in honor of Vitula, the Goddess of joy.

Young men of the Equites—the equestrian class—would gather on the Ides to process to the temple of the Dioscuri Castor and Pollux and the temple of Jupiter Optimus Maximus in commemoration of the aid of the divine twins in a battle in the early Republic. On the seventeenth, three deified personifications of virtues were honored. The double temple of Honos et Virtus—Honor and Courage—had its anniversary on the seventeenth, and there was also a sacrifice to Victory.

The eighteenth was a *dies ater*—a black day—in commemoration of the anniversary of the defeat of the Romans by the Gauls at the

Battle of the Allia in 390 BCE. The Gauls sacked the city of Rome shortly afterwards, and the date of the defeat was an unlucky day on which no business could take place.

Regular festivities resumed the following day with the Lucaria, which was celebrated on the nineteenth and twenty-first but not on the twentieth. This festival's meaning was obscure even in ancient times. Named for the large grove on the Tiber where it was held (*lucus* means "grove,") it could have been held there because the Romans sheltered in the grove after their defeat at the Allia. It could also have derived from the early days of the city, when the forests were being cleared for farmland and the spirits of the woodland needed to be propitiated.

Concordia was the embodiment of Harmony within the state and had several temples throughout the city of Rome. The oldest and largest of these in the Forum Romanum celebrated its anniversary on the twenty-second. This was used sometimes for senate meetings as well as for meetings of the arval priests, an ancient college of twelve priests that was re-instituted by Augustus. They held rites for the grain Goddess Dea Dia and maintained her sacred grove.

An ancient festival of Neptune was held on the twenty-third, followed by the Furrinalia on the twenty-fifth. This obscure holiday celebrated Furrina, a Goddess little known in historical times who had a grove with springs at the foot of the Janiculum Hill, although she also had a shrine near the city of Arpinum. Both of these holidays celebrating water fell in the middle of the period during which droughts would have been most severe. From the late republic on, there were games held in honor of Julius Caesar for the last ten days of the month, which ends with a temple anniversary of the Fortune of This Day. Take note of the following dates:

1st of the month: the Kalends of Julius

1st of the month: dies natalis of the temple of Juno Felicitas

5th of the month: Poplifugia

6th of the month: dies natalis of the temple of Fortuna Muliebris

6th–13th of the month: Ludi Apollinares

7th of the month: the Nones of Julius

7th of the month: sacrifice to Consus

7th of the month: Nonae Caprotinae

7th of the month: festival of Pales

8th of the month: Vitulatio

15th of the month: the Ides of Julius

15th of the month: Transvectio Equitum

17th of the month: dies natalis of the temple of Honos et Virtus

17th of the month: sacrifice to Victoria

18th of the month: dies ater (a black day)

19th and 21st of the month: Lucaria

20th–30th of the month: Ludi Victoriae Caesaris

22nd of the month: dies natalis of the temple of Concordia at the foot of the Capitoline

23rd of the month: Neptunalia

25th of the month: Furrinalia

30th of the month: dies natalis of the temple of Fortuna Huiusce Diei

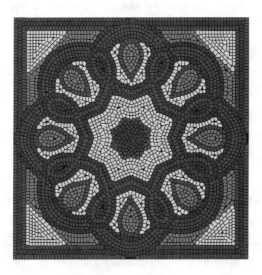

Ludi Apollinares
The Games of Apollo

During the second Punic War, the Sibylline books advised the Romans to bring the cult of Apollo to Rome, and so his worship was established in the third century BCE. His original role was to aid the Romans in war, especially as a healing God, but Apollo was also honored as a hunter, musician and poet as well as a giver of prophecies. He was particularly important to poets, who considered him the source of their inspiration. He was a Greek God imported into Rome and was never very thoroughly identified with a pre-existing Roman God, although he was associated with the Sabine Soranus as a Sun God.

The emperor Augustus was a particular devotee of Apollo and considered him his personal deity. Because he was a foreign God, his first temple—to Apollo Medicus—was outside the original precinct of the city, but Augustus built a temple to Apollo on the Palatine Hill next to his own house. This elaborate temple had numerous porches and libraries, and the Sibylline books were moved there.

Apollo's worship in Italy predated the explicit importation of his cult—he was known to the Etruscans as well, by the name Aplu, who could be a closely related God associated with Apollo or simply a version of his name. In Rome, Apollo was associated both with Neopythagoreanism and with Orphism—which included beliefs in reward and punishment after death and in reincarnation—and in these cults the God was considered the father of Orpheus and of Pythagoras. His myths were carved on coffins in both Orphic and Neopythagorean tombs.

At his games in July, everyone wore garlands to the festivities as in Greek rites. The holiday included sacrifices, chariot races, two days just for circus games, two days just for theatrical performances and six days of street fairs.

Statue of Apollo

Hymn to Apollo, excerpt

Lyre-player and teacher of the melodious Muse
Thalia,
Phoebus, you who wash your tresses in the
River Xanthus,
Slight youth Agyieus,
Defend the honor of the Daunian Muse.
Phoebus gave me the breath of inspiration,
Phoebus gave me the skill of song and the name
of poet.

You blue-blooded girls and boys
who arose from famous fathers,
under the guardianship of the Delian Goddess
bringing down the swift-fleeing lynx and deer,
keep the Sapphic rhythm, keep the beat
of my fingers,
singing solemnly of the son of Latona,
singing solemnly of the Moon increasing in fire,
favorable for crops and swiftly rolling out the
months headfirst.
Someday when you're married, you will say,
"When the cycle of generations brought back the
days of the festival,
I sang out the song loved by the Gods,
I was taught in the measures of the poet Horace."

–Horace Ode 4.6, tr. Mab Borden

Nonae Caprotinae or Ancillarum Feriae

When the Latins attacked Rome when the city was weakened by the sack of the Gauls, the enemy demanded the wives of the senators and other upper-class Romans as hostages. A slave woman named Philotis came up with a cunning plan, that the female slaves be dressed up in the fine dresses and jewelry of the most honored Roman matrons. (Roman slavery was not racially based and there were no obvious physical distinctions between enslaved and free people in this period, as they all came from Italy or nearby parts of the Mediterranean. In later periods, slaves from Rome's conquests in the North might be easily picked out by lighter colored hair, but slaves in any era could be freed or purchase their freedom, so physical features alone never determined a person's status as a slave.) There was no way for an enemy to know which women were slaves and which were free, so Philotis' ruse worked beautifully. The women were handed over in this garb, and after getting the enemy soldiers drunk and wearing them out in bed, they stole their swords and then Philotis gave the signal to the Romans at a fig tree. The Romans were victorious and the slave women were given dowries and celebrated at this festival.

Held on the seventh of the month, the name refers to the *Nones*, the day of the month and *caprificus*—the wild fig, or literally, goat fig. At the annual festival, the people rushed out the gates of the city, calling out common names as if mustering troops. Then slave women, wearing their mistresses' fine dresses, bawdily flirted with all the men and then beat one another and threw stones at each other. All the women—slave and free together—sacrificed a male goat to Juno under a fig tree that grew wild in the Campus Martius.

The runny white sap of the fig tree was offered to Juno in place of milk. The historian Varro also says that the women cut and use a branch of a wild fig tree—for what, he doesn't say.

The Goat-Fig Nones or the Feast of the Slave Women, this holiday's origin and purpose were unclear in ancient times, like so many Roman festivals. Relating to the fig and the tone of the day, the *mano fico*—the evil-warding hand sign used in ancient Rome and still seen in Italy—was called the fig hand and represented the vulva, intercourse, or both. The sexual associations of goats are well known, and all overlap with the bawdy character of the holiday.

Byzantine mosaics with fig trees and birds

Neptunalia

In the height of summer, the Romans began to concern themselves with water. From the fourth century BCE onwards, Neptune was identified with the Greek Poseidon, but the water God was ancient in Italy. Associated first with fresh water, only through his identification with Poseidon was Neptune considered a sea God. When he gained Poseidon's horse association, though, he also became identified with the grain God Consus, who was also a God of horses.

In the Greek image, the watery divinity drove the oceans in a golden chariot pulled by half-horse, half-dragon monsters, surrounded by dolphins and supple sea nymphs with floating hair. He could command the wild winds and the hungry waves that devour boats at a gulp, but when he chose, the God could calm the howling surf under his smoothly rolling wheels. Virgil describes his appearance as calmly regal, while Ovid says his face always bears a sour expression. As in Greek depictions, Neptune holds a trident in his statues.

In stories, Neptune didn't have much luck with his children. He had many offspring from many love affairs, but unlike his brother Jupiter, whose sons were heroes, Neptune's progeny had evil inclinations. He was the sire of the raging Cyclops Polyphemus and by snake-headed Medusa he fathered the fearsome giant Chrysaor. Neptune's numerous sons committed such outrages that he hid them in Pluto's underground chasms to save them from punishment.

Some ancient authors hint that Neptune was accompanied by a consort, either Salacia—a sea-Goddess who may have originally been a Goddess of fresh springs—or Venilia, a Goddess of the waters along the coast. In his temples in the Circus Flaminius and Campus Martius, Neptune received sacrifices, which could include bulls. Along with

Apollo and Mars, Neptune was one of few Gods who could have a bull offered to him as a sacrifice.

Almost nothing is known about the Neptunalia festival, but the timing of the festival is telling. It falls in the hottest part of the summer, when water is extremely important. The one detail that survives tells that worshippers built shelters out of leafy branches to keep the sun off. Because the Romans regularly made sacrifices to springs, fountains and other sources of water, it is easy to imagine that there was an element of propitiating the God of the water to stave off drought.

Horace's description of his own observance of the festival is reminiscent of modern holiday gatherings. He brings out the good wine and sets aside prudence to spend the night drinking and singing the songs of the Gods.

Horace III.28

What could be better to do on the
feast of Neptune?
Lydus, my servant, be quick and bring out the
Caecubian wine
which we've been keeping for some occasion
and press with force against wisdom's fortifications

...

We'll take turns caroling—first I'll sing of
Neptune and the green-haired Nereids,
then you'll call back on the curved lyre with a
verse about Latona
and the swift arrows of Cynthian Artemis.
The climax will be she who possesses Cnidos and
the sun-flashing Cyclades—Venus, who holidays
on Paphos, carried there by her yoked swans.
Night also will also be paid her due in song.

—tr. Mab Borden

Statue of Neptune in Lviv, Ukraine

Augustus
August, a hollow month

In 8 BCE, the sixth month of the year was renamed from Sextilis to Augustus in honor of the emperor Augustus. The Kalends sees the temple anniversary of Spes, the personification of Hope, followed two days later by a curious rite called the Punishment of the Dogs. The story goes that when the Gauls sacked the city, the watch dogs were starved from the long siege and failed to raise the alarm because the Gallic soldiers gave them meat—but the sacred geese kept at the temple of Juno did honk out a warning. In remembrance, dogs were punished and geese honored for their loyalty—to Rome. Geese were draped in gold and purple and carried through the streets, accompanied by crucified dogs. The processional route included the temples of Juventas (Youth) and Summanus, the archaic God of nocturnal thunder.

On the Nones is a festival of Salus, a personification of well-being. This was followed on the ninth by a festival for the Sun. Sol and Luna—Sun and Moon—each have festivals this month as well as a joint festival on the twenty-eighth. Sol is celebrated on the ninth as Sol Indiges, which is the anniversary of his temple on the Quirinal, where he was venerated from ancient times. This epithet means the Native Sun, indicating that he was likely a pre-Roman Sabine deity rather than a Latinized version of the Greek Helios. Luna was celebrated on the twenty-fourth and again a few days later on the twenty-eighth along with Sol.

On the twelfth and thirteenth there was a festival for Hercules Invictus (the Unconquered.) This began a cluster of festivals on the Ides, which included feasts of several Gods as well as temple anniversaries of Castor and Pollux, Hercules Victor (the Victorious) and Fortuna Equestris, the face of the Luck Goddess who protected the interests of the equestrian class. Flora had a second festival on the Ides as well, with her main celebration being in April.

Two of the festivals of the Ides involve Goddesses of childbirth. The primary one was the Nemoralia, a festival of Diana. This day also honored the water Goddesses called the Camenae who watched over the city's water supply and who were appealed to by women in childbirth. The Vestal Virgins drew the water used to ritually sprinkle the temple each day from the sacred spring of the Camenae outside the Porta Capena. When the bronze shrine there was struck by lightning, their worship was moved to the temple of Hercules Musarum because the Camenae were associated with the Greek Muses. They shared a shrine there with Egeria, a water nymph who was wife and advisor to Numa Pompilius, Rome's second king and its lawgiver who also instituted many of its religious rituals and customs. Like the Camenae, Egeria was prayed to by women in labor. At their shared shrine, the Camenae received libations of water and milk.

The last of the festivals on the Ides was for Pomona—another nymph and a Goddess of fruit—and Vertumnus, a God of seasons and orchards. Both the temple of Vertumnus on the Aventine and the nearby temple of Diana on the Aventine celebrated their anniversaries on this day. Four days later was the festival of Portunus, God of locks, doors, keys and harbors. Although strongly associated with Janus, Portunus had his own cult and temple, with his own flamen as well—the flamen Portunalis. He can be recognized in images by the keys he carries, which likely opened storerooms for the harvest as well as doors within the city. The area near his temple in the Forum Boarium was a center for florists, and the temple itself was converted into a Christian church in the ninth century—the church of Santa Maria Egiziaca, Saint Mary of Egypt. The festival itself happened on the Pons Aemilius, a bridge of unknown location.

On the nineteenth, the flamen Dialis broke unripe grapes off the vine in the Vinalia festival in honor of Jupiter and Venus. This rite concerned the grape harvest but did not coincide with it—the grapes didn't ripen until the end of September. The twenty-first is the Consualia for the grain God Consus and is followed by a festival of Ops—a Goddess of abundance—after an interval of three days. In December, this pattern will be repeated with a festival of Consus on the fifteenth and a festival of Ops on the nineteenth. Between the two in August, the feast of Vulcan on the twenty-third included sacrifices to Maia, Ops and the Nymphs of the field.

Because plants rise from beneath the Earth, Gods of grain were frequently considered chthonic powers. Somewhere in Rome— most likely on the Palatine Hill—was a pit called the Mundus Cereris (of Ceres.) Considered a gate to the Underworld, it was covered over except for three days each year—August twenty-fourth, October fifth and November eighth. The stone that closed over the pit was called the lapis manalis and when it was removed, ghosts were free to roam the city. Each of these days was considered unlucky and no business was conducted while the dead were at large.

Ending the month were the festival of Sol and Luna and the Volturnalia on the twenty-seventh. This festival honored Volturnus, a river God sometimes considered to be the father of the nymph Juturna, and sometimes identified with the Greek Eurus, the East Wind. Take note of the following dates:

1st of the month: the Kalends of Augustus

1st of the month: dies natalis of the temple of Spes (Hope) in the Forum Holitorium

3rd of the month: Supplicia Canum (the Punishment of the Dogs)

5th of the month: the Nones of Augustus

5th of the month: festival of Salus

9th of the month: festival of Sol Indiges

12th and 13th of the month: festival of Hercules Invictus

13th of the month: the Ides of Augustus

13th of the month: festival of the Camenae

13th of the month: dies natalis of the temple of Castor and Pollux

13th of the month: Nemoralia

13th of the month: festival of Flora

13th of the month: dies natalis of the temple of Fortuna Equestris

13th of the month: dies natalis of the temple of Hercules Victor

13th of the month: festival of Vertumnus

17th of the month: Portunalia

19th of the month: Vinalia

21st of the month: Consualia

23rd of the month: Vulcanalia

23rd of the month: sacrifice to Maia during the Vulcanalia

23rd of the month: sacrifice to the Nymphs in the Field during the Vulcanalia

23rd of the month: sacrifice to Ops Opifera (Ops the Bringer of Help) during the Vulcanalia

24th of the month: festival of Luna

24th of the month: opening of the Mundus

25th of the month: Opiconsivia

27th of the month: Volturnalia

28th of the month: Games of Sol and Luna

Nemoralia

Although primarily a protector of women, the Goddess Diana belonged to everyone—slave and free—and her most notable temple stood in a working class neighborhood on the Aventine, the humblest of Rome's seven hills. Diana had shrines as well as several temples in Rome, but the date of this festival coincides with the anniversary of the temple of Diana on the Aventine. That monument was raised by the king Servius Tullius, who convinced other members of the Latin League to build the temple in cooperation with Rome. In front of the temple hung a pair of cow's horns of a curious origin. One of the Sabines had a cow which gave birth to a female calf of remarkable size and physical perfection. The man brought the cow to Rome and led her before the temple of the Goddess, right up to the altar. The priest was shocked by the size and fame of the beast and asked the man why he would come with impure hands to offer a sacrifice. The priest told him to wash himself in the running water of the Tiber first and while he was bathing, the priest sacrificed the cow. Her horns were hung in front of the temple where they remained a source of awe for generations, as a signal that Rome would be blessed because one of its citizens offered up such a perfect animal.

The temple on the Aventine featured a xoanon—an archaic wooden statue of a God supposed to have fallen from heaven and which is more typically found in Greek worship. It was said that the xoanon of Diana on the Aventine resembled the cult statue of Artemis at Ephesus, and that Servius Tullius's desire to build a temple to Diana was inspired by that sanctuary. Originally an ancient Italian spirit of sacred groves and trees, Diana was identified with the Greek Artemis at least as early as 400 BCE. In later periods in the Celtic provinces, Diana was worshipped alongside the healing and hunting God Apollo Cunomaglus in England and was identified with the hunting Goddess Abnoba in the Black Forest and the boar-hunting Goddess Arduinna in the Ardennes. Diana was widely beloved in Rome and the Nemoralia was an extremely popular festival.

Her worship is older than the city of Rome, and from the time of the old Latin League, Diana was venerated at a sanctuary at Lake Nemi, which filled a volcanic crater about sixteen miles Southeast of Rome. Here she was Diana Nemorensis—Diana of the Woods—and she shared her sanctuary with the forest God Virbius and the water nymph Egeria. Diana's priest—the *rex nemorensis* or king of the woods—had to be a runaway slave who gained his office by killing the priest who served before him. The site is filled with votive offerings—miniature clay models of people or of various body parts and hunted animals.

At the Nemoralia, women donned garlands and gathered to process to the sanctuary at Nemi, bearing torches. When they arrived at the wood, sometimes crossing the water in boats led by lamplight, they gave thanks to Diana for answering their prayers. Worshippers who lived too far from Rome or from Lake Nemi needed no particular site for the summer festival. Almost any grove—pine, cedar, laurel, willow—served as a temple to this rustic deity because all such dappled places were regarded as sacred to Diana.

At the feasts on this day, even the patricians served themselves because servants and slaves were allowed the holiday. The food included roasts spitted on hazel twigs and apples still hanging in clusters from their boughs. Everyone chose a tree to decorate and from its branches hung the time-honored symbols of the

Goddess—a crescent moon, bows and arrows, silver masks, tiny animal figures, scraps of clothing, locks of hair. The emblems are diverse, but so are the aspects of this Goddess. Diana was Goddess of the moonlight and the hunt—at once celestial and sublime, earthy and bloody—patroness of women in childbirth, guardian of youth, healer, comforter of the oppressed, tamer and protector of wildlife. The rites continued until the Christian fourth century, when they were still so popular that they were not able to be shut down but were converted into a celebration of the Assumption of the Virgin.

Odes 3.22

Virgin guardian of the mountains and the groves,
When called on three times, you hear new
mothers in childbirth
and snatch them away from death,
O three-formed Goddess.
May it be yours, this pine tree that hangs
over my villa,
so that through the passing years
I may happily
give it the blood of a boar just at the age to
be considering
the first oblique blow.

—Horace, tr. Mab Borden

Festival of Vertumnus

The son of Saturn, Picus was king of a land called Ausonia. When he was not even twenty, he loved horses and hunting and was pursued by the nymphs of the forest for his good looks and his noble spirit. He rejected them all, though, because he only loved Pomona, daughter of Janus and the nymph Venilia. She was beautiful with many suitors of her own, and her voice was so lovely that the birds and forest animals would follow her when she sang, the rivers would slow down to listen, the rocks would roll along after and even the trees would track her footsteps. One day when Picus was out hunting boar, he wandered into the woods where Circe the Witch was gathering herbs to use in her enchantments. He flashed by in his crimson cloak, and even though she saw him for only a second, the daughter of the Sun was stricken with desire for the beautiful young man. The herbs fell forgotten from her hands as the fire of passion reached into her very bones. When thought returned, he was gone, but with secret herbs and incantations she summoned the image of a boar and charged it with luring the young king back to her. It rushed off and soon found the king, leading him to a dense thicket where he had to dismount, leaving his foam-flecked horse behind while he chased the phantom.

When he came into the heart of the glade where Circe waited, the Goddess propositioned him, and begged him to make a Titan his father-in-law. He spurned her, telling her he only loved the singing daughter of Janus. Her pleas turned to threats, and then to dark promises which she fulfilled. Circe turned to the West twice, to the East twice and then touched Picus three times with her wand while speaking arcane charms. In terror he ran away from her, more swiftly than he had ever run until it seemed he was nearly flying. Then he saw wings appear on his own sides as he transformed into a bird. He still haunts that forest, pecking at the bark in the woods of Latium, the crimson color of his cloak now a feathered crown, his golden jewelry a ring of bright feathers.

Pomona went on to marry Vertumnus, an Etruscan deity who personified the change of seasons. Through his association with Pomona—who was a Goddess of Fruit—Vertumnus became God of orchards and gardens. When the Romans captured the Etruscan town of Volsinii in 264 BCE, they adopted the town's God Vertumnus. He had a statue in the Forum and a temple on the Aventine, with his festival on the Ides of August.

Pomona by F. Kabiank

Vinalia and Venus

The Latin word venustus means Venus-like and poets use it to signify attractiveness, charm, grace and flirtatious charisma in anyone they wish to praise for these qualities. Its opposite invenustus means unattractive, ill-mannered and base, an invective often hurled by the same writers at objects of derision. Venus was Goddess of beauty, sex and charm. Her name relates to the Latin veneror, meaning to worship, adore or venerate, literally a ritual act of encouraging or enticing. By extension Venus rules fertility in field and garden. It is in this guise that Venus is honored at the Vinalia festival. Despite her patronage of tillers of the soil, Venus was seaborn, adopting the myths of Aphrodite, with whom she was identified.

Among her cultists Venus enjoyed the regard of both gardeners and prostitutes. Her first temple in Rome was dedicated at a Vinalia festival by Fabius, a politician who had built it from fines exacted for women's adultery. In some myths she is extremely particular, even vengeful, and in others gracious. In the myth of Pygmalion—the artist who had for so many years ignored Venus—he stumbled onto the charms of women when he accidentally fell in love with a statue of his own making. Desperately wishing for it to be real, when he finally came to the altar of the Goddess to beg for her favor and aid, he couldn't bring himself to speak the words to ask for what he really wanted. She knew his heart, though, and magnanimously granted his wish anyway, bringing the statue to life through the lover's touch.

Venus was not merely Goddess of individuals looking for love—she had an important role in the state. Venus was believed the mother of the seafaring hero Aeneas who was the ancestor of Romulus and Remus—and of Julius Caesar. Her imagery includes seashells, mirrors and doves and the Goddess' many titles indicate her roles as patron of the Julian dynasty as well as freedwomen, a changer of hearts, purifier and indulgent benefactor of hopeful lovers. Her titles do not reflect her role in agriculture, but at this festival, she is paired with Jupiter—perhaps in his role as rain-bringer—to bless the vines.

The Vigil of Venus poem excerpted below was written by an unknown author on the night before a festival of Venus, sometime before the fourth century CE.

Pervigilium Veneris

…Tomorrow Dione[1]—propped up on her
exalted throne—proclaims the laws.
The one who has never loved, let him love
tomorrow! And the one who has loved before,
tomorrow, let him love!
Then a sea from the blood of the gods, in a
frothy mass, in the midst of the azure swarms
and in the midst of the horses stepping on two
feet, brings forth Dione, quivering from the
marital rainshower.
The one who has never loved, let him love
tomorrow! And the one who has loved before,
tomorrow, let him love!

…

Born from the blood of Cyprus and from
the winds and from the purples of the Sun,
wedded only in vow, tomorrow she will not
be ashamed to show off that blush which lies
hidden, covered by a fiery robe.
The one who has never loved, let him love

---

1   Dione is a name meaning "Goddess" that is given to several ancient deities, including both Venus and the mother of Venus.

tomorrow! And the one who has loved before,
tomorrow, let him love!
The same goddess ordered the Nymphs to
go to the consecrated myrtle grove. The boy
goes along as a companion to the girls, but
nonetheless, it is not possible to believe that
Love was taking a holiday from his work,
since he'd carried his arrows with him.
Go now, Nymphs! Love has laid down his
weapons, he is idle! He was ordered to go
unarmed, he was ordered to go nude, without
any bow nor with arrows nor with anything
that injures by the fire of passion. But
nevertheless, beware, Nymphs, because Cupid
is beautiful. He's the same even when he is
nude—Love is fully armed.

The one who has never loved, let him love
tomorrow! And the one who has loved before,
tomorrow, let him love!

—tr. Mab Borden

Consualia

After Romulus raised the wall of his new city, he needed to popu-
late it, so he opened it up to outlaws who had been banished from
other Latin cities. These were almost all men, though, so they came
up with a plan to bring women into Rome. Romulus and some
members of the senate went to each of the neighboring Latin and
Sabine cities, seeking treaties and wives to help sustain the population of Rome past a single generation. No city was interested in
intermarrying with these upstarts, though, so Romulus resorted
to trickery and violence. The Sabines were the closest to Rome
and had forbidden any of their women from marrying Romans, so
the Romans invited them to a harvest festival under the guise of
establishing neighborly relations, with races and games in honor
of a horse God, either Consus or Neptune Equester. Many people
in the region were curious to see the new city for themselves and
saw little danger in attending a horse race, so they flocked to enjoy
Rome's hospitality. Once the festival was well underway, Romulus
gave a signal and the Roman men all seized the women nearest
them and ran within the walls, fighting off the Sabine men who
tried to defend their daughters. All the women were virgins—there
was only one matron among them, Hersilia. After they were all
raped by their abductors, Romulus begged the women to accept
the Roman men as their husbands, imploring the men to treat the
women gently and kindly as wives rather than captives. He himself
married Hersilia and the relations between them all slowly softened.
When the Sabines returned as an army to take back their daughters,
Hersilia led all the now-Roman women onto the battlefield, where
they begged their fathers and husbands to greet one another not as

enemies but as fathers and sons in law, ending the war. From then on, Rome was Sabine as much as Latin and many of the Sabine Gods became Gods of Rome.

In later times, the Romans kept up the festival in honor of Consus, who among other attributes was a God of secret plans. As a God of horses, Consus was associated with Neptune. Probably originally a God of seeds stored underground, Consus—whose name comes from a verb meaning "to plunge in"—was a God of the granary who was worshipped at an underground altar in the Circus Maximus. He also had a temple on the Aventine Hill, although his primary worship was at the underground site, which was only uncovered for the days of his festivals. At these rites, the flamen Quirinalis—the same priest who sacrificed to Robigus in the Spring to prevent the growth of scale mildew on the crops—performed a first fruits sacrifice in the presence of the Vestals. The festival also included chariot races, and a day of rest for beasts of burden—horses and donkeys— who were garlanded with flowers in thanks for their participation in the harvest.

Consus was also somewhat associated with the abundance Goddess Ops, with a repeating pattern in August and December of festivals of the two deities with intervals between. Ops—who was called Consiva (Sower) and Opifera (Bringer of Help) was a Sabine Goddess associated with Saturn and through his identification with Cronus she was also identified with the Greek Rhea. Ops had a temple on the Capitoline Hill.

Although the source is late and the grammar questionable, Tertullian says that the underground altar of Consus was engraved with these words:

Consus mighty in counsel, Mars mighty in war, Lares mighty in the home.

Vulcanalia

For her role in interrupting the Battle of Lacus Curtius between the Romans and Sabines, Hersilia was deified after her death. Romulus became Quirinus and Hersilia became Hora Quirini. As part of the peace treaty after the battle, the Sabine king Titus Tatius and Romulus came to an agreement to combine their kingdoms and rule them jointly. During the five years of this arrangement—which ended with the murder of Titus Tatius—the Sabine king established the worship of a number of deities who remained important in Rome long after his death. One of these was Vulcan, God of forge and fire who was also called *Mulciber* (Smelter.) He had an ancient shrine in the Forum Romanum at the foot of the Capitoline hill. This was called the Vulcanal and was attributed to Titus Tatius, and the fire God also had a temple on the Campus Martius.

His cult was very ancient and Vulcan had his own priest—the flamen Vulcanalis. Greek pottery painted with images of Hephaestus have been found in sanctuaries of Vulcan as early as the sixth century BCE, so the identification between the Gods was very ancient and their overlap was considerable. Like his Greek counterpart, Vulcan ruled the forge. In Italy, he was also identified with the Etruscan Sethlans, who shared his iconography of a smith's hammer but also ruled over craftsmanship generally. Vulcan was the patron God of Ostia, Rome's port city, and the priest of Vulcan held great sway there. On August twenty-third, Romans would rise early to begin the day by candlelight for good luck, then purchase fish that the fisherman had caught in a specific part of the Tiber called the area of Vulcan. The pater familias of each family would throw a small fish—complete with scales—into the fire. The rites also included the sacrifice of a boar and a red calf.

In the cramped quarters of the ancient city, fire was a constant danger and propitiating Vulcan was one safeguard against it. The emperor Augustus established cohorts of *vigiles*, freed slaves who watched the city by night for signs of fire and fought it wherever possible. In 64 CE a fire broke out in the rows of shops near the Circus Maximus. Thousands of vigiles carried vessel after vessel of water from Rome's nine aqueducts to try to quench the flames. When that failed, they demolished buildings to try to keep the blaze from spreading. Nevertheless, the conflagration raged for six days and seven nights. Citizens fled their homes if they were able, sheltering in tombs and other monuments. The destruction was so great that the event was called the Great Fire of Rome. Almost immediately, a rumor spread that Nero himself had ordered the fire set, although he was (conveniently) away from the city at the time. It is unlikely that Nero was involved, but he took the blame nevertheless. Pliny the Elder calls the event, "Emperor Nero's Fire" and the historian Suetonius reports that Nero watched the fire and, admiring its beauty, sang an aria about the fall of Troy. So great was the emperor's reputation for vapidity and capriciousness that it was said that he gave the order because he found the narrow, winding streets and old buildings so unbearably ugly. The emperor—who considered himself a great artist and was concerned foremost with aesthetics—did nothing to help this by rebuilding in a more fashionable style.

The Great Fire not only destroyed countless private homes, but also damaged several temples, part of the forum, and the imperial palace. Nero replaced this with his Golden Palace, raising taxes and devaluing currency to pay for it, which did not improve the emperor's reputation. Needing to shift the blame, Nero claimed that the fire had been set by Christians and launched a vicious religious persecution against the young religious community. He had Christians burned alive, crucified and killed by dogs and other animals, all as public spectacle. Saint Paul was beheaded as part of Nero's persecutions and Saint Peter was crucified upside down. The site of his death is now St. Peter's Square in the Vatican, where the emperor Constantine later constructed a basilica in his honor.

Shifting blame alone was not enough to contain the crisis. How had the Gods allowed such a great calamity? Nero and the senate consulted the Sybilline books and upon their advice, the Romans propitiated Ceres, Proserpina and Vulcan. Juno also received supplication by the married women of the city. Nonetheless, Nero's reputation never recovered and he was dead within four years. Aware of the impact a national calamity can have on a ruler's fortunes, seventeen years later the emperor Domitian erected a series of altars to Vulcan throughout Rome, as well as a new temple.

At the Vulcanalia festival, some of the offerings took place at the Vulcanal, but some were likely in the Campus Martius as well—among the deities included in the Vulcanalia sacrifices were the Nymphs of the Field. Ops Opifera also received offerings at the Vulcanalia, perhaps to protect the newly-harvested grain from the risk of fire in the hot, dry end of summer. Maia—a Goddess of growing things who was later identified with the mother of Hermes—was frequently associated with Vulcan and was also included in the sacrifices at his festival.

VVLCANVS

Imperat Æthnæis mea magna potentia fabris,
Subsidiumq̃ fero Diuis, et tela ministro.

Engraving by Nicolaes Braeu
after design drawing by Karel van Mander,

September
September, a hollow month

The seventh month of the old calendar, September doesn't have as many feriae as the summer months, but heavily emphasizes Jupiter. He is honored with a festival as Jupiter Liber as well as an offering on the Capitol on the Kalends, a temple anniversary on the Nones, two *epuli* (feasts) on the Ides—one as part of the Capitoline triad of Jupiter, Juno and Minerva—and at the Ludi Romani. Also called the Ludi Magni (Great Games,) this multi-day festival in honor of Jupiter originally celebrated a military victory. Juno is also honored as Queen with a sacrifice on the Kalends and as part of the Capitoline triad on the Ides. In later periods, there was also a cavalry parade on the following day.

The temple of Apollo Medicus in the Campus Martius was restored in 32 BCE, with its rededication on the twenty-third of September.

Afterwards, it was referred to as the temple of Apollo Sosianus after the consul Gaius Sosius who paid for much of the artwork in the new temple. Latona, the mother of Apollo and Diana, was also honored on this day.

The twenty-sixth was the temple anniversary of Venus Genetrix— Venus the ancestor of the Roman people. She was also the personal patron of one particularly influential Roman. In 50 BCE, Julius Caesar's army was preparing to face the army of the Roman Republic under the command of Pompey in the Roman Civil War. Caesar's legions were considerably outnumbered, but Caesar was such a compelling commander that even when he couldn't afford to feed his soldiers— much less pay them—they chose to stay with him when he offered to release them from their service. Caesar had a knack for commanding intense personal loyalty and it was said that he could call every man of the tens of thousands in his army by name. The patron of his family was the Goddess Venus, whom the Julian clan counted as an ancestor through Aeneas, so perhaps it was her gift of charm that lent him his great charisma. When his troops prepared to face Pompey's much larger army, though, he needed every scrap of power he could muster to overcome the odds. On the night before the battle of Pharsalus, Caesar vowed a temple to Venus Victrix (the Victor) if he should win against Pompey the Great and his more numerous legions. The next day, he routed Pompey's army so thoroughly that the scales of public opinion tipped in his favor, ultimately deciding the war and eventually resulting in Caesar's complete dominion over Rome. He fulfilled his vow to the Goddess by building a temple to Venus Genetrix rather than Venus Victrix, one of many subtle but public displays of his connection to her. It also distinguished him from Pompey, who had built a temple for Venus Victrix in the Campus Martius less than ten years prior. Caesar's temple of Venus Genetrix was dedicated in 46 BCE, with its dies natalis celebrated every year on August twenty-sixth. Take note of the following dates:

1st of the month: the Kalends of September

1st of the month: festival of Jupiter Liber

1st of the month: festival of Juno Regina on the Aventine

1st of the month: offering to Jupiter Tonans (the Thunderer) on the Capitoline

5th of the month: the Nones of September

5th of the month: dies natalis of the temple of Jupitor Stator

5th–9th of the month: Ludi Romani

13th of the month: the Ides of September

13th of the month: Epulum Jovis (Feast of Jupiter)

13th of the month: dies natalis of the temple of Jupiter Optimus Maximus

13th of the month: Epulum to Jupiter, Juno and Minerva

14th of the month: Equorum Probatio (the Approval of the Horses)

23rd of the month: dies natalis of the rededication of the temple of Apollo

26th of the month: dies natalis of the temple of Venus Genetrix

Jupiter and the Ludi Romani

Many days in September honored Jupiter, the preeminent God of the Romans. It opened with a festival of Jupiter Liber—the God as a creative force—and an offering to Jupiter Tonans—the Thunderer who recalled the Etruscan Tinia—at a temple vowed by Augustus after he was nearly struck by lightning. Undeniable in his power with lightning blazes and rolling thunder, Jupiter was the mighty king of the sky and father of the Gods. To give the supreme divinity his due, Rome celebrated him in a spectacular way for two weeks in September. But then, Jupiter is the most spectacular of the Gods, accorded pride of place in the state religion. Battle banners and military gear bristled with Jupiter's emblems, the thunderbolt and eagle. Flint—readily sparking—was among his devices and Roman priests summoned rain by rubbing a sacred flintstone. Smaller stones were used ritually to seal oaths and military treaties because Jupiter—in a moral function rare in Roman Gods—guaranteed good faith. In this role he was Jupiter Lapis (Jupiter of the Stone.) Oak trees were sacred to him because of their susceptibility to lightning and once struck, a tree was hallowed and encircled by a wall to keep off the profane.

Jupiter's nature was expansive and fruitful, so despite his association with honoring oaths, he was unfaithful to his wife at a dizzying rate (and Roman marriage was not nearly as concerned with men's fidelity as it was with women's.) His unrestrained fertility promoted the abundance of the state. The marriage of Jupiter and Juno was nonetheless extremely important to Rome— the flamen Dialis and his priestess wife tended Jupiter's shrine and both were required to observe numerous prohibitions whose origins were long forgotten. Among the multitude of bans, the priest was forbidden to knot his clothing or hair, walk under grape arbors, touch or speak of ivy, beans or female goats. He could neither touch nor name a dog. The same strictures applied to his wife and she was further forbidden to climb a ladder beyond the third rung or comb her hair on certain days.

Jupiter is frequently also called Jove in English because this is how his name was rendered in some cases in Latin. Talking about or calling on him, you would say Jupiter, but for possession, objects and other uses you would say Jove, so that in some phrases Jupiter would be rendered as Jovis or Jovem. For example, you might say "Jupiter has a temple" or "that is the temple of Jove," referring to the same structure. An archaic form of his name was Diespiter, in which "piter" is from *pater* (father) and "Dies" could refer to the sky, divinity or Zeus—meaning Sky Father, Father God or Father Zeus. This is distinct from the Underworld God Dis Pater, whose name derives from *dives* (wealthy.)

JUPITER IN ROME

Before Rome, Jupiter was worshipped at the Alban Mount as Jupiter Latiaris (Jupiter of the Latins.) His name shows up in religious inscriptions and rites of the Umbrians and the Oscans. He was a sky God with dominion over the weather—particularly storms—and was associated with trees, mountains and hills. Rome's second king Numa Pompilius erected an altar on the Aventine to Jupiter Elicius, who brought the rain. This altar also served as a place for augury. The oldest temple in Rome was that of Jupiter Feretrius on the Capitoline. This tiny temple fell into disrepair under the Republic and was restored by Augustus. It included a sacred oak tree and spoils of war and, curiously, had no cult statue—only a scepter and a flint knife for sacrificing pigs.

The chief of the Gods had many names—Jupiter Fulgur was the God of daytime lightning, a counterpart of Summanus, who hurled his bolts at night. He looked out for the military interests of Rome as Jupiter Invictus (Unconquered) and Jupiter Victor (Victorious,) and the emperor Domitian built temples to Jupiter Conservator (the Preserver) and Jupiter Custos (the Guardian.) The Palatine had a temple of Jupiter Propugnator (the Defender) and as Jupiter Stator (the Stayer,) the God prevented soldiers from fleeing before an enemy. He also defended Rome as patron of bakers—Jupiter Pistor (the Baker.) Legend tells that when Rome was besieged by the Gauls, Jupiter appeared to the Romans in a dream, commanding them to throw their most precious possessions at the enemy soldiers. Food was beginning to run out, so they ground all the grain they had left, baked it into loaves and hurled them over the walls. The Gauls took this to mean that the Romans had such a store of food that they would never be able to starve them out and so they lifted the siege. This unlikely story served to explain an altar of Jupiter Pistor on the Capitol.

The primary sanctuary of the God on the Capitoline Hill was that of Jupiter Optimus Maximus (the Best and Greatest,) who was also called Summus et Exsuperantissimus (Highest and Most Supreme) after Eastern influence. This form of the God was so popular and common that his name Jupiter Optimus Maximus was commonly abbreviated to "I.O.M." His ancient temple on the Capitoline was vowed by the Roman king Tarquin, but there was one problem—the site was already occupied! The other deities worshipped there had to be moved and the only God who refused to make way was Terminus the God of boundaries, whose shrine was incorporated into the new temple, with part left uncovered because Terminus must be under the open sky. It was dedicated on September 13, 509 BCE by the first consul of the Roman Republic. In the early Republic on the

Ides of September, a state magistrate would hammer a nail into the wall of the sanctuary of Jove to ward off evil, a rite similar to one the Etruscans carried out in the temple of their God of fortune. A triple temple, it served all three deities of the Capitoline triad—Jupiter, Juno and Minerva with three sanctuaries side by side, each with its own hearth. Jupiter's was in the middle and housed a terracotta cult statue of the God with a thunderbolt. Minerva's sanctuary was to the right and Juno's to the left. All three were adorned with gold coffered ceilings and gracious mosaic floors. Victorious generals would dedicate spoils of war to the temple so that it was filled with trophies of Rome's greatness. This temple served as the center of Roman state religion and was so frequently struck by lightning that it had to be repaired and rebuilt numerous times.

JUPITER IN THE PROVINCES

As Rome expanded, Jupiter's name and his thunderbolt spread in all directions, marching alongside his eagle emblem carried by the Roman army. Rome always retained its military character, its piety and its value of loyalty to state before self but it also changed as it grew and Romanness became a broad cultural identity that incorporated many of the philosophies, legends, traditions and religions of the various peoples its conquests brought into the fold. This was no adulteration because there was never a pure form of Roman religion—it was always a syncretism of various earlier Italian religions and the tendency to cross-identify similar deities continued as Rome outgrew Italy. Because the Romans themselves readily associated their Gods with those of other peoples, these syncretisms should not be considered un-Roman in any way by the modern reader.

The best-known of these associations is also the closest. Jupiter was quickly identified with the Greek Zeus—their powers and iconography overlapped so precisely that Jupiter completely absorbed the mythology of Zeus. This led to his identification as the son of Saturn and the Greek wealth of stories expanded Roman understanding of who Jupiter was. Jupiter changed shape a bit in the North as well— the people in the Celtic Roman provinces adopted many Roman Gods including Jupiter, identifying them with their own deities in a particular form of religion that was simultaneously Roman and Celtic. In the territories of the Lingones, Mediomatrici and Treveri tribes, a large number of Jupiter columns were erected, which could reach a height of nearly fifty feet. They had inscriptions dedicating them to Jupiter and Juno and often had ornamentation suggesting a tree. They were topped with sculptures that included a figure who looks much more like a Celtic Sky God than Jupiter—he has snake arms and wears armor while riding on horseback down a mountain, wielding a lightning bolt with a Sun-wheel as a shield. This wheel was a common Celtic symbol of the Sun. The solar association does not undermine the identification with Jupiter—in Rome, Jupiter brought light as Jupiter Lucetius, a name which predates the founding of the city.

Jupiter would often take the names of Gods he was identified with as epithets of his own name. In the Alps, he had sanctuaries as Jupiter Poeninus (the name of a local God) that dated back before the founding of Rome and in what is now Austria, Jupiter was called Jupiter Uxellinus after a local mountain God. In Sicily, he was popular as Jupiter Milichius (Gracious Jupiter,) a God of abundant crops who derived from the Greek Zeus Meilichios. In Spain, there were inscriptions to Jupiter Digus and Jupiter Ladicus—combinations of Jupiter with local mountain Gods. In Turkey, he was combined with the weather and sky God Dolichenus and together they became Jupiter Dolichenus, who wielded an axe along with a thunderbolt, wore a military uniform and who was a God of the universe and success. This cult in turn came back to Rome, and Jupiter Dolichenus had temples on the Esquiline and Aventine Hills. In the city of Heliopolis in Syria, he was identified with the thunder God Hadad and a temple of Jupiter Heliopolis was raised on the Janiculum Hill in Rome.

Jupiter Optimus Maximus was particularly popular in the provinces. In Gaul, there were inscriptions to Jupiter Optimus Maximus Beissirissa and Jupiter Cernenus. The Best and Greatest was popular in Spain as well as Dacia and Pannonia (areas overlapping with modern Transylvania and Western Hungary and Slovakia) and the Partheni tribe in Dacia made him their own and worshipped him as Jupiter Parthinus.

In Spain, Jupiter Optimus Maximus was associated with a local God named Geius, with the inscription, "I.O.M. Geius." A similar inscription in England reads, "Jupiter Optimus Maximus Tanarus," which is probably a misspelling of the thunder God Taranis, who reportedly received human sacrifices.

THE LUDI ROMANI

Jupiter Optimus Maximus was honored by the Romans on many occasions, but his major holiday was the multi-day Ludi Romani in September. The timing of the holiday was crucial. For farmers, field and orchard demanded little attention in September. For the military, campaigns wound up and soldiers marched home. The throng converged on Rome—relaxed from labor and battle, the populace was now in a serious mood for pleasure.

Like Jupiter's other festivals, the Ludi Romani began with a *pompa*, a lavish parade. Whatever magistrate was putting on the show went first—this could be an aedile, praetor or consul—dressed in the garb of a victor. Next came the sons of any citizens who were eligible for military service, with the sons of the Equestrian class riding on horseback to reflect their anticipated military rank. The children were not yet old enough to join up, but played at soldier for the festival. Entertainers for the circus followed—barely-clad wrestlers and boxers, charioteers and all those who competed for the pleasure of the crowd. After these pranced the flute players and the *ludiones*—the dancers whose role was so essential that if any stopped dancing, the entire parade would halt and have to be started over from the beginning. The three groups of ludiones—children, teenagers and men old enough to join the army—all dressed up as soldiers in blood-red tunics with the belts, spears and short swords of the Roman infantry. The martial character of their performance extended to the dances themselves, with each group of ludiones dancing in formation, following the steps of their leaders in moves that evoked the thrusts, strikes and parries of the battlefield. The mood was lightened by jesters with hair standing up straight, decked in flowers in place of scarlet and goatskin belts in place of the soldiers' bronze. Their dance was a comic mockery of the steps of the ludiones. Behind them were the musicians, playing flute and lyre and bringing up the rear were people carrying incense, the fragrant clouds preparing the atmosphere for the very last bit of the show—statues of the Gods carried through the streets by citizens.

Before any of the contests could begin, cows were sacrificed to the Gods, with Jupiter holding prize of place. Entertainments followed—during the course of the holiday were dramas and comedies, puppet shows, clowns, acrobats, boxing, foot races on oiled animal skins and chariot races. Sports for the autumn festival and other major celebrations evolved into the notorious Coliseum games, so shockingly brutal that they have virtually eclipsed from history the profoundly religious character of ancient Rome. And of all worship, the Jupiter cult was the most imposing. Beyond his supreme status as the Father of the Gods, for Romans he exemplified the grandeur of the state itself. As Jupiter was simply Best and Greatest, so was Rome.

Jupiter embracing Cupid after Raphael's fresco in the Chigi
Gallery of the Villa Farnesina in Rome

Juno

While September was dominated by the Ludi Romani and the rites of Jupiter, Juno, too, received offerings and was included in the rituals of the month with festivals on the first and thirteenth. She also had a festival on the Kalends of July and the Kalends of every month was sacred to her. An ancient Goddess, the wife of Jupiter was from early times associated with the Etruscan Uni, a Goddess of women, marriage and fertility. Uni was part of a triad sharing a temple with Tinia and Menrva, who in Rome were associated with Jupiter and Minerva, respectively—the other Gods of the Capitoline triad. Juno was also identified with the Greek Hera, and the tales of Juno as the rabidly jealous wife exacting ruthless revenge on hapless women come from this association.

The name Juno is related to words for youth and fertility, and she bore a number of cult titles indicating her power over marriage and fecundity, for example Juno Pronuba (First Bride or Honored Matron,) Juno Interduca (Who Leads the Bride into Her Marriage,) Juno Domiduca (Who Leads the Bride to her New Home,) Juno Cinxia (Who Loosens the Belt) and Juno Pomana (of Fruit.) When girls first reached puberty, the Goddess protected them as Juno Sororia and in childbirth she protected them as Juno Opigena (the Daughter of Ops.) Other titles indicate a more celestial nature—Lucetia (lightbringer) and Virgo Caelestis (Heavenly Maiden.)

As Juno Caelestis, she was associated in Carthage with the fertility Goddess Tanit. Under Roman rule, Juno Caelestis became the patron deity of the city and she presided over an oracle there. She was also associated with light as Juno Lucina—an epithet that means "of the grove" but that was so similar to the Latin word for light (*lucis*) that the Goddess was linked with it. This form was another in which she protected women in childbirth—bringing newborn babes into the light. Women calling upon Lucina unbound their hair and any knots in their clothing, to remove any barrier that might prevent a child coming forth. The Vestals hung locks of their hair in a sacred grove at the temple of Juno Lucina on the Esquiline Hill and the king Servius Tullius ordered that a coin be placed on her altar for every child born in Rome.

A pre-Roman Latin Goddess, Juno Regina (the Queen) was first persuaded by the general Camillus to abandon her home city of Veii and come instead to Rome, where he built her a temple on the Aventine. Eventually Juno Regina had multiple temples in Rome and as part of the Capitoline triad, she had a particular role as protector of Rome. Soldiers offered to her as Juno Curitis (of the Spears) and the curiae (tribes) held feasts where they sacrificed first fruits, grain and wine in her honor. From the earliest days of the city, she was Juno Populona (of the People Assembled for War) and the infantry continued to worship her under this title. Because of its relation to the word for "people," this epithet was also responsible for the growth of the Roman population. After the sacred geese at her Capitoline temple honked out a warning that the Gauls were attacking the city, Juno was called Moneta (the One Who Warns.) In another legend, on an occasion when there had been an earthquake, a voice called out from her temple to tell the Romans to sacrifice a sow. The same temple on the Capitoline was also a treasury.

Juno Sospita (Savior) and Juno Sispes Mater Regina (Juno Savior, Mother, Queen) came to Rome from the Latin town of Lavinium at the same time the Latin League was dissolved. Juno Sispes was a fierce protector of Rome with a particularly martial appearance. She appears wearing a goat skin with head and horns intact as a helmet, carrying a shield and spear, standing in a chariot and accompanied by a snake, raven or crow. The shift in the location of her worship symbolized the complete domination of Rome over the other Latin cities.

October
October, a full month

The month opens with the flamens of Jupiter, Mars and Quirinus—the original Capitoline triad—riding in a covered cart drawn by horses to the temple of Fides on the Capitoline Hill, where laws scribed on bronze plaques hung on the walls. There the priests made sacrifices with their right hands draped in white cloth. The Goddess of Trust who ruled oral contracts, Fides was very ancient and her cult was among those instituted by Rome's second king Numa Pompilius. It was said that she was older than Jupiter and she was depicted as a white-haired old woman. Her imagery is recognized by the emblem of covered hands.

Also on the Kalends is the Tigillum Sororium, with the Bacchanalia beginning a few days later. October is the month of the grape harvest, which began a few days prior at the end of September, revealing how disconnected the Roman religious calendar was from agricultural cycles. While it is easy to imagine rustic fairs with barefoot youths stomping the juice from the grapes, laughing and tipsy with the previous year's product, that sort of festival is purely an invention of the post-industrial imagination which longed for a romanticized past. The timing of the Bacchanalia in October might at first seem to support such a fantasy, but that holiday does not seem to have anything to do with the grape harvest, and instead was part of a mystery cult whose rituals—which did have a reputation for including drunkenness—were held privately rather than being a state-sponsored celebration and could be held at other times of year as well. The only rite the Romans celebrated this month concerning the vintage is the Meditrinalia on the eleventh. That ritual involves tasting the wine and honors Jupiter and a Goddess named Meditrina. She was possibly invented by later Romans to explain the existence of the holiday, but there is almost no information about this rite and none at all about her.

The fourth and fifth were both sacred to Ceres. First was a day of fasting called the Ieiunium Cereris. This was done every five years in honor of the grain Goddess, but was made an annual observance by Augustus. On the fifth, the Mundus of Ceres was opened for a second time and ghosts were free to roam the city. The following day was a *dies ater*—a black day of mourning in remembrance of the massive defeat of the Romans by the Teutoni and Cimbri tribes at the battle of Arausio in 105 BCE.

Jupiter and Juno each had rites on the Nones, with a festival in the curiae for Juno and one at the roofless temple of Jupiter Fulgur (Jupiter of Daytime Lighting) in the Campus Martius. Two days later, there were sacrifices to three Gods who looked after the interests of the people of Rome. The first was to Genius Publicus

Populi Romani (the Communal Spirit of the Roman People,) who appears in art as a man in Greek dress, holding a cornucopia or later as a crowned, bearded man holding a globe and scepter along with the cornucopia. The second was to a Goddess of Good Luck named Fausta Felicitas and the third to Venus Victrix (the Victor.) This was followed the next day by the temple anniversary of Juno Moneta, who warned Rome of attacking enemies.

On the twelfth, there were elaborate games in honor of the emperor Augustus that included sacrifices to Fortuna Redux as well as contests of many kinds. Augustus instituted them in his lifetime and they continued as part of the new imperial cult after his death. Between the Augustalia and the Ides are the Fontinalia—which honors springs and is also called the Festival of the Source—and the anniversary of the rededication of the temple of the Di Penates on the Velian Hill. While the Penates were primarily household divinities associated with ancestor worship, they had a public cult as the ancestral spirits of the Roman People in which they were called Penates Publici Populi Romani (the Penates of the Common Roman People.) Legend held that these public Penates were brought by Aeneas from burning Troy to Rome.

There were two festivities on the Ides—the Capitoline Games which were privately sponsored games put on by the priests of Jupiter rather than a state festival, and the sacrifice of the October Horse for Mars. On the nineteenth, in an official end to the season of military campaigning, the weapons of the army were purified in the Armilustrium on the Aventine Hill. In a ritual similar to the March rites, the Salii priests of Mars danced around the weapons with their sacred shields before they were put away for the winter.

The month ended with the Victory Games of Sulla, which were established in 81 BCE to celebrate Sulla's victory over the Samnites. In honor of the Goddess of Victory, they were originally called the Ludi Victoriae.

This festival continued through the Kalends of November. Take note of the following dates:

1st of the month: the Kalends of October

1st of the month: festival of Fides

1st of the month: ceremony of the Tigillum Sororium

3rd–7th of the month: Bacchanalia

4th of the month: Ieiunnium Cereris

5th of the month: Opening of the Mundus

6th of the month: *dies ater* (a black day)

7th of the month: the Nones of October

7th of the month: offering to Juno Curitis

7th of the month: offering to Jupiter Fulgur

9th of the month: sacrifices to Genius Publicus, Fausta Felicitas and Venus Victrix

10th of the month: dies natalis of the temple of Juno Moneta

11th of the month: Meditrinalia

12th of the month: Augustalia

13th of the month: Fontinalia

14th of the month: dies natalis of the temple of Di Penates

15th of the month: the Ides of October

15th of the month: Capitoline Games

15th of the month: sacrifice of the October Horse to Mars

19th of the month: Armilustrium

26th of the month: Kalends of November Ludi Victoriae Sullanae

Tigillum Sororium

When Rome's legendary third king Tullus Hostilius went to war with Alba Longa, both cities knew that a war between them would create an opportunity for the Etruscans to attack. To prevent this threat, Tullius Hostilius made an agreement with the Sabine ruler that each city should put forward three champions who would fight to the death to decide the outcome of the war. The Romans were represented by the three triplets of the Horatian family, called the Horatii and three triplets called the Curiatii stood for Alba Longa. The two cities were close neighbors and Camilla, the sister of the Horatii, was engaged to one of the Alban Curiatii brothers. Nonetheless, each had his duty and they took to the field.

In the fight, two of the Horatii fell first, and only one brother—Horatius Publius—stood against the Albans. Two of the Curiatii were wounded, but the odds were still in their favor. Publius turned and ran, discarding the appearance of courage in favor of a clever ploy—because of their wounds, the pace of each of the Curiatii brothers was different, so by forcing them to pursue him, Publius Horatius spread his enemies apart, allowing him to take them on one at a time. As soon as he halted and turned, he immediately attacked his first pursuer, taking him by surprise and killing him. He ran to meet the second of the Curiatii—who was injured and winded—and killed him as well. The last and most gravely wounded Alban brother knew he stood little chance against Publius but faced him squarely anyway. The final Horatius brother called out that he had killed the first two Curiatii to avenge his brothers and that the last, he killed for Rome. Then he ran his sword through his enemy's throat, winning the day for the Romans. He stripped the Albans of their armor and carried it back to the city as a prize.

No sooner had he entered within the walls, though, than Camilla saw that the bloodstained spoils her brother carried included a cloak that she had made for her betrothed with her own hands. She fell to her knees, wailing in grief, to which her brother responded by thrusting his sword through her heart, killing her on the spot and declaring that no Roman woman should ever grieve for Rome's enemies. The slaying of kin was an unforgiveable crime and Publius Horatius was condemned to death. To plead his cause, Publius addressed an assembly of the people and his father also begged the common people of Rome to spare him the grief of seeing his last child die after three had already been slain for Rome. The people were moved by the old man's plea and voted to let Publius live under two conditions. Because a pater familias was responsible for the actions of everyone in his family, the father had to make sacrifices in atonement for his son's crime. Publius also had to pass under a wooden beam—the sister's beam. Passing under the yoke was a sign of submission in war and symbolized Publius submitting again to the laws of Rome.

Altars to Janus Curiatus and Juno Sororia were raised under the beam, which remained for many generations after the legendary events and was periodically replaced. When soldiers returned from war, it was walking under the beam that recalled them to civilian life. In remembrance of Publius and Camilla, the ritual of the sister's beam was enacted at the end of the campaigning season on the Kalends of October.

Bacchanalia

A Greek priest came to Rome from Etruria and began initiating Roman women into the secret mysteries of Bacchus. They conducted initiations for other women three times a year, and at first only women could join the new priesthood. Eventually, though, initiation was extended to young men and the triannual daytime rites became nocturnal banquets occurring five times each month. From this arose an underground society of drunken orgies peppered with spontaneous prophetic possession in which men thrashed and contorted as they were overtaken by the spirit of the God. Married women would unbind their hair and dress as Bacchantes—the manic followers of Bacchus wearing revealing dress and carrying the thyrsus, a symbol both vegetative and phallic. They carried torches to the Tiber, where they would reveal the miracle of the flames continuing to burn after being dunked in the river—a cheap showman's trick caused by the chemical composition of the torches, which was not unlike Greek fire.

Aside from the fact that this religious fanaticism was of a type that ran directly against traditional Roman morality and social standards, the cult of Bacchus was not all in good fun. Members worked together to further their own political and material advantage, assassinating rivals, offing relatives and falsifying their wills, presenting false evidence at trials and conspiring to disgrace the children of the wealthy so as to blackmail their parents. Sworn to secrecy, anyone who spoke of the rites or these other crimes simply disappeared and fellow initiates were told that they were carried away by the Gods. In this way, the secrets were kept until 186 BCE, when the testimony of a prostitute brought the whole ugly business to light and the senate made the cult illegal.

A young Equestrian man named Aebutius of about sixteen years old was living on the Aventine Hill with his mother Duronia and his stepfather Rutilus, who had been a very poor guardian to the boy. Aebutius would soon reach his majority, and at that time he could call his stepfather to account for his treatment. Rutilus needed a way to prevent this, so he conspired with the boy's mother to have him initiated into the cult of Bacchus, which would surely involve enough disgrace to give Rutilus something to hold over him. That is, if the boy survived—Aebutius seemed the type to try to cry foul of the whole business. Duronia quietly pulled her son aside one day and told him that when he was a very young child, he had been gravely ill with a fever and that she had promised the Gods that she would have him initiated into the Bacchanalian mysteries if only he would recover. Now that he was on the verge of attaining the toga of manhood, she must see her vow fulfilled. Aebutius agreed and his mother gave him instructions to abstain from sex for ten days and cleanse himself with water. Then she would lead him to the shrine where he would be initiated.

Aebutius' mistress lived right next door, so he went to explain to her why he would be avoiding her company for the next while. A Spanish woman named Hispala, she had been brought to Rome as a slave and worked as a prostitute. While her mistress kept the majority of that income, slaves could customarily make tips and so eventually Hispala saved enough to buy her freedom. As a freed-woman, she continued in the trade she knew and eventually became a very well-renowned courtesan. She took a liking to the young Aebutius, however, and never charged him any fees. He was even the heir in her will. When she was still a slave, Hispala herself had been initiated into the mysteries alongside her mistress and knew what a dangerous situation her lover was in. She begged him not to do as his mother had asked and exacted a promise from him that he would not be initiated. When the young man told his mother and stepfather that he had changed his mind and would not be initiated after all, they kicked him out of the house.

Aebutius went to stay at his aunt Aebutia's house and told her the whole tale. She recommended that he take the story to the consul Postumius, which he did. The consul listened to the boy's story and found it credible enough that he decided to inquire delicately into the cult. He enlisted the help of his mother-in-law Sulpicia because she was well-connected in the neighborhoods of the Aventine and was the kind of Roman matron who was above suspicion. Sulpicia assured him that Aebutia was an honest woman and arranged to have Aebutia drop by when Postumius happened to be visiting her home. In this way, the consul was able to maintain discretion and avoid any complications that might have arisen from public knowledge of his investigation into the cult of Bacchus. Postumius and Aebutia chatted, and the consul eventually brought the conversation around to the woman's nephew. She broke down in tears and told him the entire story of why she had taken the young man in.

Satisfied with this first witness, Postumius asked Sulpicia to see to it that he could meet Hispala and see what she had to say about the matter. This was more difficult, because there was no social circumstance under which a respectable woman and a freedwoman courtesan would encounter one another casually and she certainly could not just invite her over. She could, however, summon her to appear before her—superior to inferior—and this she did. Hispala fretted because did not know why she was summoned but she appeared nonetheless and when she arrived at Sulpicia's house, the consul was waiting in the vestibule, along with the lictors carrying the *fasces*—the bundles of rods and axe that symbolized the authority of the state to punish or execute a citizen. He led the now terrified courtesan into the back of the house where Sulpicia waited, and Hispala gathered herself together. When Postumius' questioning turned to the mysteries, though, she began to shake—she had sworn secrecy, after all, and feared the wrath of the Gods. She was more afraid of the consul, though, when the anger rose in his face, and she confessed everything to him. She told him not just of the licentious rituals and orgies but also of the various crimes the initiates had conspired to commit. Fearing that cult members would make the witnesses disappear, Sulpicia hid Hispala in her own home and Postumius arranged for a loyal friend who owed him a favor to protect and conceal Aebutius.

When the whole story was aired before the senate, the horrified populace generously rewarded both Aebutius and Hispala with money,

Young Bacchus

granting the former his majority and waiving his military service, and providing Hispala with a dowry and giving her the right to marry any man without bringing dishonor to him or his family, removing legal if not social barriers. The senate banned the cult of Bacchus and from then on, when a neighbor heard drum or cymbal and drunken shouts from another apartment on the crowded Aventine, they responded with suspicion rather than annoyance.

This story comes from a later historian but the text of the ban from 186 BCE indicates suppression rather than eradication and mostly focuses on doing away with the secret society aspects rather than the religious ones. Specifically, it bans oaths and pledges, funds held in common, centralized leadership and male priests within the cult. In response, there was a widespread persecution throughout Italy that resulted in destruction of the original Etruscan cult grotto, which featured an underground chamber with a terracotta sculpture of a throned Bacchus with a leopard at his feet. That the cult survived, though, there is no doubt. A villa in Pompeii called the Villa of the Mysteries includes a room richly decorated with murals running around all four sides. All on a red background, the scenes include images of Bacchus reclining in a woman's lap, Silenus with a wine bowl and Satyr attendants holding a mask, a kneeling nude woman drawing a veil back from an object that is obscured and another woman kneeling while behind her stands a winged female figure wielding a whip. These scenes may depict a Bacchic initiation, teasing the viewer with unexplained details that can never now be understood—or they may be simply decoration.

Tales of the Bacchantes—the most extreme of which depict the frenzied followers roving the countryside performing feats of superhuman strength and tearing to pieces any person who crosses their path—are designed to shock and enrage but the cult's appeal was not limited to drunken licentiousness. Like other Roman mystery cults, it likely offered a glimmer of hope for an afterlife. In the early empire, Bacchus' image and stories can be found on the coffins of his initiates. This stood in contrast to the generally vague and dark Roman views of death. At best, you might live on as a shade in the realm of Orcus, haunting the streets of the city a few days each year, hoping some relative left out a few scraps. Some tombstones indicate that the deceased hoped to reunite with family in the Underworld, but many Romans don't seem to have believed in any kind of existence after death at all or are ambiguous about it. *Memento mori* (remember that you will die) was a common saying that served as a reminder to enjoy life while you can because soon the light will go out. A common inscription on Roman tombs reads *NF F NS CN,* which stands for *non fui, fui, non sum, non curo*—usually translated to mean "I didn't exist, I did exist, I don't exist, I have no cares." While this is a realistic assessment of the limited human understanding of death, it also seems a poor reward for enduring the difficulties of life. In contrast, the various mystery cults that took hold in Rome— Bacchism, the rites of Magna Mater, the Eleusinian mysteries into which many Romans were initiated, the cult of Isis and eventually Christianity—all contained themes of death and regeneration. Through personal identification with these stories, the individual initiate gained access to some kind of hope of a meaningful afterlife and relief from the terror of the grave. They are each different cults, though, with many distinctions from one another.

The Bacchanalia in particular provided in its mysteries a release from the strictures of society, with Bacchus himself—the ever-growing grape—representing the triumph of nature over human order. Closely identified with Dionysus and carrying all the phallic associations of the Greek rites of the God, Bacchus offered his followers a mystic ecstasy which could be attained in the present.

Song of the Bacchantes, Ode 3.25

Where are you snatching me off to, Bacchus,
since I am full of you?
To what groves or grottos
will I be driven, swift with a new mind?

...

No differently does a sleepless Bacchante
stand speechless on a ridge, looking out
at the Hebrus River and Thrace sparkling
with snow
and at the Rhodope mountains, traversed all over
by her uncivilized feet,
just as it pleases me when I wander to admire
untouched riverbanks and lonely forest glades.
O Master of the Naiads,
and of the Bacchantes strong enough
to pull up the lofty ash trees with their hands.
I will sing nothing trivial or in a humble rhythm,
nor will I speak about anything of a mortal nature.
It is a sweet danger, O Lenaeus[1],
to follow a God, wreathing my brow
with green vine-leaves.

–Horace, tr. Mab Borden

---

1   Lenaeus is a name for Bacchus meaning "of the wine press."

Fontinalia

Janus and Juturna had a son named Fons or Fontus who was God of springs and wells. The Romans honored him on October thirteenth by hanging wreaths and garlands around wells and throwing them into springs. Fons had a temple in Rome near the Porta Fontinalis—a gate named for a nearby spring—and an altar on the Janiculum Hill. Although other sources describe only garlands, Horace writes of an offering he made to a spring called Bandusia which was on the property of his country villa.

Ode 3.13

O Bandusian spring, more glittering than glass,
worthy of pure, sweet wine and not without flowers,
tomorrow you will be presented with a kid
whose brow is just swelling with the first horns.
He is fixed on love and battle,
but in vain. For this progeny of the lustful herd
will color the icy stream with red blood, for you.
Even the dreadful hour of the blazing Dog Star
is unable to touch you—you offer your pleasant
coolness to
bulls weary from the plow
and to roving herds.
You also will be among the famous springs,
because I am telling of the holm oak growing
on the hollow in the rock
where your babbling waters run down.

–Horace, tr. Mab Borden

Sacrifice of the October Horse

Just as the military season began with horse races in March, so it ended in October, with a chariot race and the uncommon offering of a warhorse.

The festivities began with a two-horse chariot race in the Campus Martius. Of the winning pair of horses, the horse on the outer side of the track was offered to Mars. The flamen Martialis killed the animal with a spear—a weapon sacred to Mars.

As soon as the horse fell, its tail was cut off and a runner carried it straightaway to the Regia, where the still-warm blood was dripped on the hearth. The blood from the tail of the horse was gathered up by the Vestals, who kept it until the following April when they mixed it with the ashes of the unborn calf slain at the Fordicidia on April 15th. They used that mixture at the Parilia on the 21st in the purification rites in honor of the shepherd God Pales. While it had an entirely separate country ritual, in the city version of the festival, the Vestal priestesses would sprinkle the mixed blood and ashes onto a fire made of bean stalks with the pods removed. Anyone who came to the festival could be purified by leaping through the flames of this fire three times and be cleansed with pure water sprinkled from a bay leaf.

After the sacrifice in the Campus Martius, the horse's body was beheaded and the head was draped with loaves of bread. The men of two neighborhoods—the Via Sacra and the Subura—battled fiercely for this prize. In years when the men of the Via Sacra won, they hung the head from the wall of the Regia, and when the men of Subura won, they placed it on the Mamilian Tower, a monument that was in their neighborhood.

Vintage painting of Venus and Bacchus

November
November, a hollow month

Farmers spent the month of November plowing and sowing to prepare the fields for winter wheat, and so there were very few festivals during this month. Two festivals overlap the beginning of this month—the victory games of Sulla and a festival of Isis. Gaining prominence in later periods, the cult of Isis had a lesser festival in March but its major celebration started on the last day of October and continued through the first three days of November.

On the fourth, Romans began the Plebeian Games in honor of Jupiter. These featured chariot races and other entertainments in the Circus Maximus, and were second only to the Ludi Romani. As part of the festivities, there was a banquet in honor of Jupiter on the Ides. All the senators would attend and feast after sacrificing a white heifer. In the midst of the games was a moment of pause as the Mundus was uncovered for the third and final time of the year on the eighth, allowing the manes—spirits of the dead—to pass into the world of the living for a day.

A festival on the Ides of November is for Feronia, a Goddess of Spring who was associated with Flora and Libertas—the personification of freedom. The festival was held in the Campus Martius where Feronia had a grove and temple, but the Goddess was more broadly worshipped in Etruria and in other Latin towns in the region than she was in Rome. Her shrines were favored by slaves, freedwomen and plebeians (many of whom had freed slaves in their ancestry.) Feronia's temple in Terracina was a site for the manumission of slaves as well as a place where slaves could seek sanctuary. Slaves would be manumitted at public events where there were plenty of officials and witnesses—events such as games. This festival occurred near the Circus Flaminius where the Plebeian Games were originally held before they moved to the Circus Maximus, so the festivals may have been connected.

Also on the Ides was a festival of Fortune of the Firstborn, with an inspection of the cavalry on the following day.

Take note of the following dates:

1st of the month: the Kalends of November

October 31—November 3: Festival of Isis.

1st of the month: Ludi Circenses (end of the Ludi Victoriae Sullanae)

4th—17th of the month: Ludi Plebeii (Plebeian Games)

5th of the month: the Nones of November

8th of the month: Opening of the Mundus

13th of the month: the Ides of November

13th of the month: festival of Feronia

13th of the month: festival of Fortuna Primigenia

13th of the month: Epulum Jovis

14th of the month: Equorum Probatio

Festival of Isis

Everyone wore white in the procession of Isis. Women in shining white dresses donned garlands of flowers and led the parade, carrying large bouquets in their arms and scattering flowers as they went. A large number of people followed—both men and women—carrying lamps, candles and torches to represent the stars of the night sky. Behind the lamps walked the musicians, playing sweet songs on flutes and pan-pipes, and a chorus of boys in white clothing singing hymns. There were throngs of initiates—veiled women whose hair had been anointed with oil and men whose heads were completely shaved—all wearing pure white linen and carrying sistrums, shaking them as they walked along.

Behind these paced the priests bearing the symbols of the Gods. The first carried a lamp, the second an altar which was called a source of help, the third gilded palm branches and a caduceus. The fourth carried an image of an outstretched, deformed left hand as a symbol of justice and a breast-shaped golden pouring vessel filled with milk. Behind him came a priest bearing a gilded winnowing basket and one with a wine jug. Last of all came the Gods themselves, dressed and masked for all the people to see—Anubis with a black and gold face carried a caduceus in his left hand and a palm in his right. Hathor as an upright cow rode on the shoulders of a priest. At the very end walked two priests, one holding a box containing sacred objects of the mystery cult and another carrying an image of Isis which was neither animal nor human shaped but was said to inspire awe as a symbol of a deeper meaning than any ordinary image could convey.

This description of a Spring procession of Isis comes from the second century novelist Apuleius. While his tale is mostly a fantastical romp, he was himself an initiate of the mysteries of Isis and there is no reason to think he fictionalized that aspect of his story. The details of the November festival of Isis have been lost, but some elements were likely repeated.

The worship of Isis came to Rome around 100 BCE after becoming prominent in Egypt under the Greek rulership of the Ptolemies. Because Isis and Osiris were sister and brother, the first Ptolemy promoted worship of the Goddess in justification of the practice of sibling marriage. From Egypt the cult of Isis spread throughout the Mediterranean to the many nations the Egyptians traded with. It was not initially well-received in Rome. As an initiatory mystery religion with a priesthood that was not controlled by the state religion, it was looked on with suspicion by the senate. Soon the cult was banned and there were decrees ordering the destruction of shrines of Isis in 59 BCE and again in 58, 53, 50 and 48. It was hard to find anyone willing to risk the anger of a God, though, and on one occasion the consul took an axe to the door of the temple himself because no workman would do the job.

In the second half of the cult's first century in Rome, the second Triumvirate (Octavian, Mark Antony and Lepidus) gave their authorization for the construction of a temple of Isis and Serapis. During his subsequent love affair with Cleopatra, Antony identified himself with Osiris and his beloved with Isis. Octavian (later named Augustus) defeated them and gained sole control of Rome and, needless to say, he was not a supporter of the cult. Augustus' successor Tiberius banned all Egyptian worship in Rome and destroyed a public shrine of Isis, forcing the priests of the Goddess to burn and destroy all religious artifacts and clothing. Twenty-four years later, the emperor Claudius built a temple to Isis on the Campus Martius. This was called the Iseum and it was accompanied by the Serapeum, a temple to Serapis, a newer form of Osiris.

When he came to power over Egypt, Ptolemy I promoted the worship of the new God Serapis, who was a combination of Osiris with the sacred Apis bull housed in Memphis. This God was outside the influence of fate, performed numerous miracles and ruled healing, the sky and the Underworld. Serapis was identified with many different Roman and Greek deities including Jupiter but was worshipped in Rome under his own name and is in one instance called Serapis Polieus—Serapis of the City. His images were usually bearded and borrow iconography from the Greek Hades, with Serapis enthroned

Pompeii temple mural of Isis and devotee

and holding a scepter in one hand with a three-headed dog at his knee. In Rome, the Iseum and Serapeum were both decorated with obelisks and Egyptian-style sculptures.

Isis herself was a great deal more expansive than any deity in traditional Roman religion. She was a complex but loving and compassionate Goddess whose spheres of influence included women, marriage, childbirth, newborns, fertility, crops and the harvest as well as the safety of her initiates both on land and at sea. She was also called Mistress of the House of Life and was seen by her Roman worshippers as a first ground of being—a numinous source of life from which the material and spiritual worlds emanate. She was not a creator like Ra or Amun, but it was believed within her cult that it was from her that all the other Gods came and that her name pointed to the true nature behind all the other Goddesses. Her rites involved ritualized grieving and searching for her dead son—a departure from Egyptian tradition in which it is Osiris whom she searches for—and then exulting when he is found. Images of Isis in Rome show the Goddess nursing Horus and holding a sistrum or bucket of water from the Nile. Her clothing is bound with an ankh and she is crowned with the disk of the Sun surrounded by horns or the crescent Moon.

Of the initiation into her mysteries, Apuleius furnishes the best description. His character interrupts the procession described above and then goes on to become initiated. He describes the parts of the ritual that he claims were not held secret by oath. The preparatory rites involved a sacrifice, being read instructions from sacred books, purification by bathing, a presentation of the initiate before a statue of the Goddess and a ten-day fast from meat and wine. The initiation itself took the entire night, beginning just after the stars came out, when other initiates gave him gifts and clothed him in linen. Of what came after, he claims that all he can say is that he approached the very edge of death and

then returned through each of the Elements to worship face to
face each of the Gods above and below the Earth. In the morning, the new initiate was made to look like a statue of the Sun
by being draped in twelve sacred shawls and mounting a wooden
dais in front of the temple statue, bearing a torch in his right
hand and crowned with palm branches arranged to look like solar
rays. This was followed by a feast and two days of celebration.

Prayer to Isis, *Metamorphoses* Book 11

*Blessed and eternal protector of humankind who is always generous in
nurturing mortals, indeed you bestow the sweet affection of a mother on the
calamities of the wretched. Neither day nor restful night nor any moment
no matter how quick passes without your kindness, you who protect men
at sea and on the Earth. Brushing away the storms of life you extend
your saving right hand with which you unravel even the impossibly tangled
knots of Fate and soothe the storms of Fortune and restrain the harmful
movements of the stars. The heavenly Gods worship you, the infernal
powers heed you. You spin the orb of the Earth, you set the Sun alight,
you rule the world, you crush Tartarus beneath your heel. The stars answer
back to you, the seasons return for you, the Gods rejoice and the Elements
serve you. At your command the winds blow, the clouds nourish the Earth,
seeds sprout and the seedlings grow. The birds passing through the sky, the
wild beasts wandering the mountains, the serpents laying hidden in the
ground, the monsters swimming in the depths of the sea—all tremble at
your majesty. But I know that my talent is not adequate to sing out your
praises...therefore I will take care to do the only thing the impoverished but
devout person is able to do in any case: I will picture to myself your divine
face, keeping your most holy presence stored safe away forever in the secret
places of my heart.*

—Apuleius, tr. Mab Borden

Isis from Villa Adriana

December
December, a hollow month

With sowing completed, farmers in the vicinity of Rome turned to other pursuits in December. They might plant bulbs to flower in the Spring, spread manure beneath the olives or tend to pruning and other off-season tasks. On the Kalends, patrician women in the city of Rome gathered in the private home of a high-ranking official for the nocturnal Bona Dea festival. This was followed by a festival of Faunus at his temple on the island in the Tiber on the Nones. This island saw a second festival on the eighth when the God of the Tiber River was honored at the festival of Tiberinus Pater (Father Tiber.) Two legends claim that a man named Tiberinus drowned in the river and that it was renamed after him. The first tells that King Tiberinus was a scion of the royal house of Alba Longa and a descendant of the hero Aeneas. He was killed by the river, which was called Albula at that time. The second legend gives a more divine origin for the *numen* of the river, claiming that Tiberinus was a son of the God Janus and the nymph Camasene, but maintains that he was mortal and that he drowned in the water that bears his name.

Three days later is another festival connected to Aeneas. When the legendary ancestor of Romulus and Remus died, he was buried in the banks of the River Numicus. The water of the river God cleansed all mortality from this son of Venus and he became fully divine, taking on the name Jupiter Indiges. On the same day, sacrifices were offered on each of Rome's seven hills for the Septimontia festival. The last day before the Ides was a temple anniversary of the grain God Consus, probably to celebrate the conclusion of fall sowing. He also had a second Consualia festival on the fifteenth, which included races and a day of rest for farm animals, just as at the first Consualia in August.

Between the two days on which the Romans honored the divine protector of the granary, they honored two other deities connected with agriculture, with a banquet for Ceres and a festival for Tellus (Mother Earth.) Both were held on the Ides. A lectisternium was a rite of supplication in which the images of the Gods—in this case the Grain Goddess—were laid out on couches in the style of Roman dining. At other festivals, Tellus received offerings of spelt cakes and a pregnant sow, but the details of her December festival are not known.

The spectacular seven-day Saturnalia festival began on the seventeenth and continued through the twenty-third, overlapping with most of the rest of the rites in the month. The first of these was the festival of Epona on the eighteenth. Many Roman Gods were worshipped in the provinces, but only one Gallic deity was venerated in the city of Rome. The horse Goddess Epona originated in eastern Gaul but spread to the Roman provinces in Britain, Africa and Dalmatia as well as to Rome itself. Her images always included horses and could also feature grain, fruit, a dog, a key and a flag used to signal the start of horse races.

This was followed by Opalia, a festival of the sowing Goddess Ops. This may have been connected to Saturnalia, or like the festivals of Consus, Ceres and Tellus, been related to the end of the sowing season. Two days after the Opalia, the Romans celebrated the Goddess Angerona in a festival called Angeronalia, Divalia or Divalia Angeronae. A Goddess of secrecy depicted with a finger over her mouth in a shushing gesture, the Romans petitioned Angerona to relieve anxiety and pain. Her festival involved a sacrifice in the Curia Acculeia as well as at a statue of Angerona that was housed in a shrine of Volupia, Goddess of pleasure. Her statue there shows her with her mouth covered by a gag.

Several temples have anniversaries during Saturnalia. The Lares Permarini protected sailors and had a temple in the Campus Martius. On the twenty-third is the temple of Juno Regina (the Queen) in the Circus Flaminius—also in the Campus Martius—which was next to the temple of Jupiter Stator. The temple of the Tempestates—Weather Goddesses—may have had its anniversary on this day, or it may have been on the Kalends of June. The same day marked the end of Saturnalia with the Sigillaria festival and also honored Acca Larentia at the Larentalia festival.

Several legends surround the name Acca Larentia. In one tale, she is the wife of Faustulus, the shepherd who found Romulus and Remus, making her the foster-mother of the founder of the city. The twelve Arval priests were descended from the twelve sons of Acca Larentia. In another story, she was a girl whom Hercules won as a prize in a dice game against his own temple custodian. He eventually gave up the girl, who married a very wealthy Etruscan man. Her husband died shortly after their wedding, leaving Acca Larentia several large tracts of land which she in turn left to the people of the city of Rome upon her own death. This origin story serves a political purpose by justifying Rome's claim to some of its Italian territory.

The month closes out with two final festivals from the eastern part of the Roman empire on the twenty-fifth. The first is the Brumalia celebration of the Winter Solstice which happened only in the eastern territories of Rome. This festival had a chthonic character and honored Ceres, Bacchus and other Gods of agriculture. The second is the birthday of the Unconquered Sun—that is, of the God rather than his temple. This began as a cult of the Syrian Sun God El Gabal and spread across the Roman empire, nearly replacing other forms of Sun worship in Italy. Sol Invictus came to the city of Rome in the second century CE with Elagabalus—the emperor Marcus Aurelius Antoninus, who was part of the Severan Dynasty. He had served as a priest of El Gabal as a child and when he became emperor, he brought a sacred stone with him and raised two temples to Sol Invictus in Rome. The festival on December twenty-fifth was so popular that it could not be eradicated under Christian rule and was converted to a celebration of the birth of Christ, who was frequently identified with Sun Gods in the early period of Roman Christianity. Take note of the following dates:

1st of the month: the Kalends of December

3rd of the month: Bona Dea Festival

5th of the month: the Nones of December

5th of the month: festival of Faunus

8th of the month: festival of Tiberinus Pater

11th of the month: Agonalia for Jupiter Indiges

11th of the month: Septimontia, the Festival of the Seven Hills

12th of the month: dies natalis of the temple of Consus

13th of the month: the Ides of December

13th of the month: Lectisternium for Ceres

13th of the month: dies natalis of the temple of Tellus

15th of the month: Consualia

17th–23rd of the month: Saturnalia

18th of the month: Eponalia

19th of the month: Opalia

21st of the month: Divalia, also called Angeronalia

22nd of the month: dies natalis of the temple of the Lares Permarini

23rd of the month: dies natalis of the temple of Juno Regina

23rd of the month: dies natalis of the temple of the Tempestates

23rd of the month: Sigillaria, the last day of Saturnalia

23rd of the month: Larentalia

25th of the month: dies natalis of Sol Invictus

25th of the month: Brumalia

Bona Dea Festival

Bona Dea, the Good Goddess, was a fertility Goddess identified with Fauna and she had ears only for the prayers of women. Perhaps the divinity's discrimination resulted from her treatment by the God Faunus who was either her father or husband. In one story, Faunus lusted for his daughter Bona Dea. He had her drink wine, but she refused him. Then he beat her with myrtle but she still refused him. Eventually he slept with her in the form of a snake. In another version, she was his wife and was chaste and modest as a Roman wife was expected to be. She took a sip of a wine jug out of curiosity, though, and that led to another sip and another until she was thoroughly drunk. Enraged to find her in such a state, Faunus beat her to death with myrtle sticks. In both versions, Faunus feels great remorse afterwards and grants Bona Dea divinity.

Although the Good Goddess had a temple on the Aventine Hill, her annual celebration took place in the home of a praetor or a consul—an official who possessed the authority of *imperium* (command.) While the sacrifice was offered on behalf of the Roman people, it was not a public rite and men were forbidden from attending. The magistrate's wife performed the ceremonies along with the Vestals in a room decked with flowers and vines—but not with myrtle, which was hateful to the sight of the Good Goddess. The women used wine in the ceremony, but it was referred to as milk and its large storage jar was called a honeypot. A sow was her typical sacrifice and there may have been one offered at this ceremony.

In 62 BCE, the rites were held in the home of Julius Caesar, who at that time held the offices of both praetor and Pontifex Maximus. He and all male servants left for the evening while his wife Pompeia hosted the Vestals and the women of prominent families. That year, a patrician man named Clodius Pulcher—who was noted for his good looks—dressed as a female musician and snuck into the ceremony. He was caught and only escaped with the help of a serving girl. The evening was a disaster and the rites themselves had to be repeated by the Vestals.

Rumor had it that Clodius was having an affair with Pompeia and everyone assumed that seeing her was his motive. He was vulnerable to legal prosecution, both for the adultery—fidelity to his own marriage was irrelevant but sleeping with the wife of another patrician was a crime—and for violating the sanctity of the rites. He was charged before the senate for the latter and he gave the simple defense that it couldn't have been him because he'd been out of town. Unfortunately, Cicero had chanced to run into him in Rome the very same evening and reluctantly testified against him, making an enemy of the powerful Clodii clan in the process—a move that would eventually result in Cicero's temporary banishment from the city. Clodius was acquitted and while Cicero waited out the years of his exile, Clodius Pulcher saw to it that Cicero's overpriced home— he was a bit of a social climber and had married rather than inherited his money—was razed to the ground. To satisfy his spite, Clodius had a temple to Libertas (Freedom) erected on the spot so that the house could never be rebuilt. Cicero referred to this temple as a shrine to License.

As for the charge of adultery, Caesar never took him to court and scrupulously defended Pompeia, claiming she was innocent in the matter. He did, however, divorce her, and when asked why, gave the famous response that Caesar's wife must be above suspicion. The ceremonies of Bona Dea began as a respectable and orderly affair, but Clodius Pulcher may have been ahead of his time—in the imperial period they had a reputation for debauchery.

Festival of Faunus

The rites of Faunus were performed naked because the God hated clothes. In one story, clothing deceived him and led to his humiliation. When Hercules was serving out his sentence as a maidservant, he attended his mistress and her other servants as they journeyed into the mountains to worship Bacchus. Faunus spied them from a distance and immediately desired the young woman. The party camped for the evening in a cave and Hercules and his mistress exchanged clothing—he stretched the stitches of her delicate tunic and she donned his lionskin and took up his club. They each went to their beds in this garb and in the dead of night Faunus crept into the cave, bent on having his way with the beautiful woman. When he touched the lionskin, he recoiled, fearing to wake Hercules, and went to the other sleeping figure. He lifted the tunic and just as he was getting started, the hero pushed him off. Chaos followed as the servants scrambled for lights, but when they saw Faunus laying there—shoved so hard by Hercules that he could scarcely get up—they laughed.

Other myths show a more serious side to the God, who could be appealed to for oracles and prophetic dreams as well as to protect the sheepfold. Faunus came into the city of Rome in 196 BCE with the construction of his temple on the Tiber Island. As a horned half-goat with a lustful nature, he was identified with the Greek Pan but had his own ancient cult in Italy and one of his myths claims that he was one of the mythical early kings of Latium.

His festival fell two days after the rites of Bona Dea, his sister or wife. This holiday was celebrated in many places in Italy and was more of a countryside festival—sometimes called the Faunalia Rustica—which did not appear on urban calendars. Faunus protected the herds and on the Nones of December, he blessed them. The ceremonies also included the sacrifice of a kid as well as offerings of incense and wine, after which all those present joined in dancing.

Eclogue I

I Faunus, sprung from the aether, I who
protect the ridges and the forests,
I sing to the people of those things that
will come—
it pleases me to carve on the sacred tree the
happy songs in which fate is revealed.
Rejoice above all, you farmers who dwell in
the woods,
Rejoice, o my people!
The entire herd is allowed to wander away and
its guardian remains untroubled.
The shepherd neglects to close up the stalls at
night with a wickerwork gate of ash wood,
but nevertheless no pillager will bring an
ambush to the sheepfold,
or drive off the mules in loose halters.
With untroubled peace, the Golden Age is
born again.

—Calpurnius Siculus, tr. Mab Borden

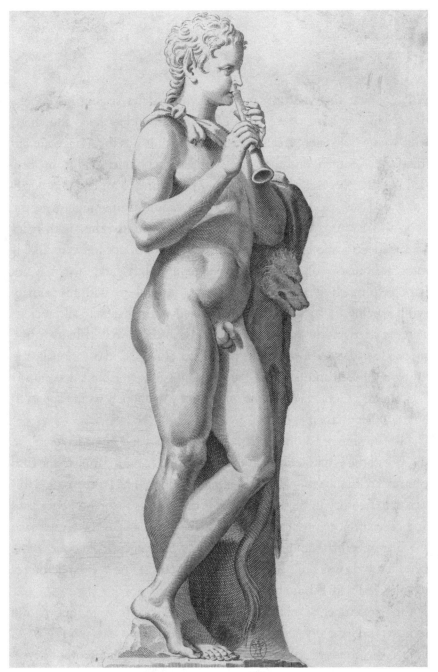

Illustration of a of a faun playing a flute

Saturnalia

When Jupiter threw Saturn out of Olympus after seizing his father's throne, the old King of the Gods came to Italy and founded a town on a hill that would later be called the Capitoline. It was the *Mons Saturnius* (the Hill of Saturn) and the town was Saturnia, which had to be fortified because the Golden Age of peace had come to an end and neighbor feared neighbor. Saturn discovered agriculture and taught it to the people of Latium, becoming the region's first king. This myth relies on the identification of Saturn with the Greek Kronos but very little is known about the cult of Saturn outside of his holiday, and there may not have been much of one. He was a God of agriculture with his primary symbol being the sickle, but he also ruled more generally all precious things placed inside the Earth—sleeping seeds as well as hidden treasures. He had vague associations with other Gods, called occasionally the husband of Ops and father of Picus and possibly worshipped alongside Lua Mater, a Goddess of plague which her worshippers would appeal to her to inflict on their enemies.

The worship of Saturn in Rome was very old and he had a temple at the foot of the Capitoline hill in the Forum Romanum dating to the fifth century BCE, the very early days of the Republic. The Romans used this as a state treasury in the Republican period and as a storehouse for laws and other important state documents. Even older than the temple was the altar of Saturn standing in front of it, which legend told either came from Troy or was built by Hercules. The cult statue was made out of wood, filled with oil and wrapped and tied with wool.

On December seventeenth, the woolen bonds were untied and removed and the cry "Io Saturnalia" rang out for a day and night. As long as the bonds remained loosened, a festive mood hung over the city.

There was a public sacrifice at the temple on the first day, followed by a public feast open to everyone. The sacrifice was conducted in the Greek style—with the head uncovered. Senators and Equestrians could wear togas to the sacrifice but took them off for the feast, removing a symbol of status as part of the inversion of hierarchies that ruled the festival.

Rome's most popular holiday was originally celebrated as a single day, then stretched over seven days, was reduced to three by Augustus and then eventually extended to five. However long the carnival atmosphere reigned, it was as if all Rome was struck by madness. There was a holiday sense of well-being and wishing joy upon your neighbors, gambling was officially permitted, everyone ate rich food, students were let out of their classes, no one worked and slaves could say what they chose with no fear of reprisal.

The role reversals that began with the open public feast extended into the private observations of the holiday over the following days, with masters waiting on slaves and being treated as equals and everyone wearing *pillei*—soft caps usually only worn by free men. Laughter and reckless spending were everywhere. Each family would sacrifice a young pig and enjoy visits with friends, exchange gifts and play games. Candles were common presents, along with *sigillaria*—little images and figurines made of terracotta or sweet, edible pastes. Each family chose a member to serve as a mock king over the festivities in their home, which altogether were viewed as a re-enactment of the Golden Age that Saturn had ruled.

Saturnaliam by Ernesto Biondi

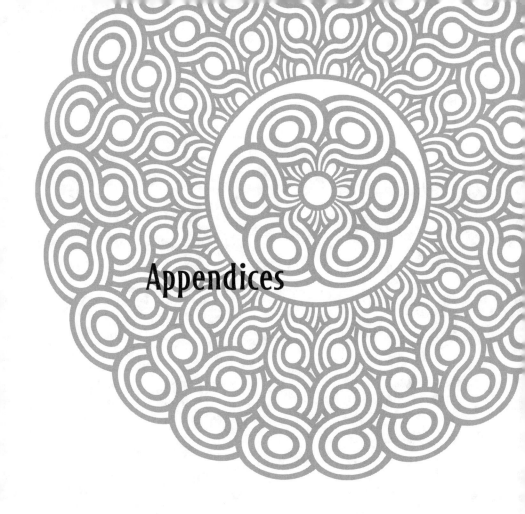

Appendices

Appendix I
Festivals by Associated Deities

Appendix II
Priesthoods

Appendix I
Festivals by Associated Deities

AESCULAPIUS

Dies natalis January 1

AGDISTIS

Ludi Megalenses April 4–10

ALERNUS

Sacra on February 1

ANGERONA

Angeronalia December 21

ANNA PERENNA

Festival of Anna Perenna March 15

APOLLO

Ludi Apollinares July 6–13
Dies natalis September 23

ATTIS

Ludi Megalenses April 4–10

BACCHUS

Bacchanalia October 3–7 (moveable)
Brumalia December 25

BELLONA

Dies natalis June 3

BONA DEA

Dies natalis May 1

Bona Dea Festival December 3

CAMENAE

August 13

CARNA

Festival of Cardea June 1

CARDËA

Festival of Cardea June 1

CARMENTA

Carmentalia on January 11

Carmentalia on January 15

CASTOR AND POLLUX

Dies natalis January 27

Ludi Castores January 27

Transvectio Equitum July 15

dies natalis August 13

CERES

Feriae Sementivae January 24–26

Cerealia April 12–19

Ambarvalia, moveable feast in May

Opening of the Mundus August 24

Ieiunium Cereris October 4
Opening of the Mundus October 5
Opening of the Mundus November 8
Lectisternium for Ceres December 13
Brumalia December 25

CONCORDIA
Dies natalis February 5
Dies natalis July 22

CONSUS
Sacrifice July 7
Consulia August 21
Dies natalis December 12
Consualia December 15

CRANAE
Festival of Cardea June 1

CYBELE
Ludi Megalenses April 4–10

DIANA
Nemoralia August 13

DI MANES
Parentalia February 13–21
Lemuria, May 9, 11, 13

DI INFERI
Feralia, February 21

Taurian Games, moveable feast in June
Terentine Games, every 100 years
Opening of the Mundus August 24
Opening of the Mundus October 5
Opening of the Mundus November 8

DIS

Feralia, February 21
Taurian Games, moveable feast in June
Terentine Games, every 100 years
Opening of the Mundus August 24
Opening of the Mundus October 5
Opening of the Mundus November 8

DIUS FIDIUS

Dies natalis June 5

EPONA

Eponalia December 18

FAUNUS

Festival of Faunus February 13
Festival of Faunus December 5

FAUSTA FELICITAS

Sacrifice to Fausta Felicitas October 9

FERONIA

Festival of Feronia November 13

FIDES

Festival of Fides October 1

FLORA

Floralia April 27
Sacra May 3
Festival of Flora August 13

FONS

Fontinalia October 13

FORTUNA

Dies natalis April 1 (Fortuna Virilis)
Dies natalis April 5 (Fortuna Publica)
Dies natalis May 25 (Fortuna Primigenia)
Dies natalis June 11
Festival of Fortuna June 24 (Fors Fortuna)
Dies natalis July 6 (Fortuna Muliebris)
Dies natalis July 30 (Fortuna Huiusce Diei)
Dies natalis August 13 (Fortuna Equestris)
Augustalia October 12 (Fortuna Redux)
Festival of Fortuna November 13 (Fortuna Primigenia)

FURRINA

Furrinalia July 25

HERCULES

Dies natalis June 4 (Hercules Custos)
Dies natalis June 29 (Hercules Musarum)
Festival of Hercules August 12–13 (Hercules Invictus)
Dies natalis August 13 (Hercules Victor)

GENIUS PUBLICUS
Sacrifice to Genius Publicus October 9

HONOS
Dies natalis of the temple of Honos et Virtus July 17

ISIS
Festival of Isis October 31—November 3

JANUS
Agonalia on January 9

JUNO
Dies natalis January 1 (Juno Sospita)
Matronalia March 1 (Juno Lucina)
Dies natalis June 1 (Juno Moneta)
Dies natalis July 1 (Juno Felicitas)
Ancillarum Feriae July 7
Festival of Juno September 1 (Juno Regina)
Epulum for Jupiter, Juno and Minerva September 13
Offering to Juno October 7 (Juno Curitis)
Dies natalis October 10 (Juno Moneta)
Dies natalis December 23 (Juno Regina)

JUPITER
Feriae Jove March 15
dies natalis April 13 (Jupiter Victor)
Vinalia April 23
Feriae Latinae, moveable feast in April (Jupiter Latiares)
Feriae Jove May 15
Dies natalis June 27 (Jupiter Stator)

Transvectio Equitum July 15 (Jupiter Optimus Maximus)
Vinalia August 19
Festival of Jupiter September 1 (Jupiter Liber)
Offering to Jupiter September 1 (Jupiter Tonans)
Dies natalis September 5 (Jupiter Stator)
Ludi Romani September 5–9
Epulum Jovis September 13
Dies natalis September 13 (Jupiter Optimus Maximus)
Epulum for Jupiter, Juno and Minerva September 13
Offering to Jupiter October 7 (Jupiter Fulgur)
Meditrinalia October 11
Capitoline Games (October 15)
Ludi Plebeii November 4–17
Epulum Jovis November 13
Agonalia December 11 (Jupiter Indiges)

JUTURNA
Juturnalia on January 11

JUVENTAS
Supplica Canum August 3

LARA, THE SILENT GODDESS
Parentalia February 13–21

LARES
Compitalia, moveable date in January
Parentalia February 13–21
Terminalia February 23
Kalends of May (Lares Praestites)
Sacra June 27

Dies natalis December 22 (Lares Permarini)

LIBER
Liberalia March 17

LUNA
Dies natalis March 31
Festival of Luna August 24
Games of Sol and Luna August 28

LUPERCUS
Lupercalia February 15

MAIA
Sacrifice August 23

MAIORES
Lemuria, May 9, 11, 13

MARS
Equirria February 27
Feriae Martis March 1
Dies natalis March 1
Equirria March 14
Agonalia March 17
Tubilustrium March 23
Dies natalis May 14 (Mars Invictus)
Dies natalis June 1
October Horse Sacrifice October 15
Armilustrium October 19

MATER MATUTA
Matralia June 11

MEDITRINA
Meditrinalia October 11

MENS BONA
Dies natalis June 8

MERCURY
Mercuralia May 15

MINERVA
Quinquatria March 19
Quinquatrus Minisculae June 13–15
Dies natalis June 19
Epulum for Jupiter, Juno and Minerva September 13

NEPTUNE
Neptunalia July 23

NYMPHS IN THE FIELD
Sacrifice August 23

OPS
Sacrifice August 23
Opiconsivia August 25
Opalia December 19

PALES
Parilia April 21

Festival of Pales July 7

PENATES
Terminalia February 23
Dies natalis October 14 (Di Penates)

POMONA
Festival of Vertumnus August 13

PORTUNUS
Portunalia August 17

PROSERPINA
Feralia, February 21
Taurian Games, moveable feast in June
Terentine Games, every 100 years
Opening of the Mundus August 24
Opening of the Mundus October 5
Opening of the Mundus November 8

QUIRINUS
Quirinalia February 17
Robigus
Robigalia April 25

SALUS
Festival of Salus August 5

SATURN
Saturnalia December 17–23

SOL

Games of Sol and Luna August 28
Festival of Sol Indiges August 9

SOL INVICTUS

Dies natalis (of the God) December 25

SPES

Dies natalis August 1

STRENIA

Kalends of January

SUMMANUS

Dies natalis June 20
Supplica Canum August 3

TELLUS

Feriae Sementivae January 24–26
Fordicidia April 15
Dies natalis December 13

TERMINUS

Terminalia February 23

TEMPESTATES

Dies natalis June 1
Vediovis
Dies natalis January 1
Dies natalis March 7
Festival of Vediovis May 21

Dies natalis December 23

TIBERINUS PATER
Festival of Tiberinus Pater December 8

VENUS
Veneralia April 1 (Venus Verticordia)
Vinalia April 23
Vinalia August 19
Dies natalis September 26 (Venus Genetrix)
Sacrifice to Venus October 9 (Venus Victrix)

VERTUMNUS
Festival of Vertumnus August 13

VESTA
Kalends of March
Vestalia June 7–15

VICA POTA
Dies natalis January 5

VICTORIA
Sacrifice July 17
Ludi Victoriae Sullanae October 26–November 1

VIRTUS
Dies natalis of the temple of Honos et Virtus July 17

VITULA
Vitulatio July 8

VOLTURNUS

Volturalia August 27

VULCAN

Feriae of Vulcan May 23
Ludi Piscatori Junne 7
Vulcanalia August 23

Appendix II
Priesthoods

AUGURS

The college of augurs interpreted thunder, lightning and flights of birds for omens. Originally there was one augur from each of the three original tribes under Romulus, but eventually the number grew to sixteen.

ARVAL BROTHERHOOD

These twelve priests were selected from the most influential patrician families. They were responsible for maintaining the fertility of the fields by propitiating Gods of agriculture and were particularly dedicated to Bona Dea. They tended her sacred grove a few miles South of Rome, which had both a temple and bathhouse. During the imperial period, the emperor was always a member of the Arval Brotherhood and these priests also carried out some of the rituals of the imperial cult (worship of deified emperors.)

DUUM VIRI

Originally these were only two men, one patrician and one plebeian. Eventually their number expanded to fifteen but they were always half from patrician and half from plebeian families. Also called the Sacris Faciundis, these priests consulted and interpreted the Sibylline books.

FETIALES

These were twenty priests from the patrician class who acted as diplomats to treat with other nations. They declared war by throwing a spear and oversaw ceremonies related to ensuring that a war was just. The head priest of the Fetiales was called the Pater Patratus.

FLAMENS

Priests dedicated to a specific God were called flamens. Their role was to tend the temple and make offerings to that God. The three most important flamens were the priests of the original Capitoline triad—the Flamen Dialis (priest of Jupiter,) flamen Martialis (priest of Mars) and flamen Quirinalis (Flamen of Quirinus). They were subject to many taboos but could hold political office. The others were considered minor flamens who served relatively obscure deities. The identity of two Gods who had a flamen in their service is unknown. Altogether there were fifteen flamens before the empire, assigned to these thirteen deities: Carmentis, Ceres, Falacer, Flora, Furrina, Jupiter, Mars, Palatua, Pomona, Portunus, Quirinus, Volturnus and Vulcan. Once the imperial cult came into being, flamens were added to serve the deified emperors. The flamen Augustales served the deified Augustus, the flamen Divorum served all the deified emperors.

FLAMINICA DIALIS

The wife of the flamen Dialis had her own ritual duties to the cult of Jupiter which included regular sacrifice and the maintenance of personal taboos. She maintained her office until the death of her husband.

HARUSPICES

A haruspex was a person who interpreted signs in the entrails of animals and also in lightning and events which were considered unnatural. They were not an organized college like the augurs until the imperial period.

LUPERCI

The priests of the Lupercalia were divided into two colleges founded in legend by Romulus and Remus. These were called the Quintilii and the Fabii, respectively.

PONTIFICES

A pontifex was a priest who could serve in rituals and sacrifices to many Gods, in contrast to the duties of a flamen to a particular deity. The obligation of the flamen was to the God, whereas the obligation of the pontifex was to the state, to maintain its religious obligations. Their duties included determining the dates of religious festivals, maintaining funerary laws and a number of primarily administrative tasks such as recording the most important events that occurred in a year. This college of priests was the most important in Rome, entirely controlling state religion. It began as a patrician organization of only three members but over time expanded to include plebeians with a total of sixteen priests. From the late republic on, these were elected positions.

PONTIFEX MAXIMUS

The head of the college of pontifices oversaw the other priesthoods. He was chosen through a popular election until the imperial period, when the emperor served in the role.

REX SACRORUM

The pontifex maximus appointed this priest to fulfill the role of the king in religious ceremonies after the end of the monarchy. He was forbidden from holding any political office. His wife was called the regina sacrorum and also had religious duties.

SALII

The twelve dancing priests of Mars had two colleges—the Palatini and the Collini. The Palatini were dedicated to Mars Gradivus (Marching.) The Salii performed leaping dances with shields and carried swords and spears.

SODALITES

The collective term for the minor brotherhoods of priests was the sodalites. These brotherhoods included the Fetiales, the Salii and the Arvals as well as the Titiales who were appointed by king Titus Tatius to keep up Sabine rituals as well as priests appointed to the cults of Augustus and Hadrian after their deifications.

VESTALS

The priestesses of Vesta were under the authority of the Pontifex Maximus. They watched over the sacred flame of Vesta and maintained her hearth, and also guarded sacred objects and made certain sacred cakes. Most priesthoods were for life, but the Vestals served thirty years under strict chastity, after which they could marry if they chose.

The small temple of Augustus

Select Bibliography

Adkins, Lesley, and Roy Adkins. *Dictionary of Roman Religion*. New York: Oxford University Press, 1996.

———. *Handbook to Life in Ancient Rome*. New York, NY: Facts On File, 1994.

Apuleius, Lucius Madaurensis. *The Golden Ass*. Translated by P.G. Walsh. Oxford: Oxford University Press, 2008.

Beard, Mary, John North, and Simon Price. *Religions of Rome*. Volume 2, a Sourcebook. Cambridge: Cambridge University Press, 1998.

———. Religions of Rome: Vol. 1 a History. Cambridge: Cambridge University Press, 1998.

Bodel, John, and Saul M Olyan. *Household and Family Religion in Antiquity*. John Wiley & Sons, 2012.

Brandt, J. Rasmus, and Jon W. Iddeng. *Greek and Roman Festivals: Content, Meaning, and Practice*. Oxford: Oxford University Press, 2012.

Dupont, Florence. *Daily Life in Ancient Rome*. Translated by Christopher Woodall. Oxford, UK: Blackwell, 1989.

Feeney, D. C. *Caesar's Calendar: Ancient Time and the Beginnings of History*. Berkeley: University of California Press, 2007.

Fowler, W. Warde. *The Roman Festivals of the Period of the Republic*. Pantianos Classics, 1899.

Garland, Robert. "Greek and Roman Priests and Religious Personnel." Oxford Research Encyclopedia of Religion, April 5, 2016. https://doi.org/10.1093/acrefore/9780199340378.013.25.

Graf, Fritz. "Festivals in Ancient Greece and Rome." Oxford Research Encyclopedia of Religion, May 9, 2016. https://doi.org/10.1093/acrefore/9780199340378.013.58.

Grant, Michael. *Roman Myths*. New York: Scribner, 1971.

Habinek, Thomas N. *The World of Roman Song: From Ritualized Speech to Social Order.* Baltimore: Johns Hopkins University Press, 2005.

Horatius, Quintus Flaccus. *The Complete Odes and Epodes.* Translated by David West. Oxford: Oxford University Press, 2000.

———. Horatius, Quintus Flaccus. *Horace in His Odes.* Edited by J.A. Harrison. Wauconda, IL: Bristol Classical Press, 1981.

Hornblower, Simon, Antony Spawforth, and Esther Eidinow. *The Oxford Classical Dictionary.* 4th ed. Oxford: Oxford University Press, 2012.

Jörg Rüpke, and David M. B. Richardson. Pantheon: *A New History of Roman Religion.* Princeton, New Jersey: Princeton University Press, 2018.

Livius, Titus. *Hannibal's War: Books Twenty-One to Thirty.* Edited by Dexter Hoyos. Translated by John Yardley. Oxford: Oxford University Press, 2009.

———. *History of Rome,* Books 1-5. Translated by Valerie M. Warrior. Cambridge, MA: Hackett Publishing Co, Inc, 2006.

Maccius, Titus Plautus. *Plautus: The Pot of Gold, and Other Plays.* Translated by E.F. Watling. Harmondsworth: Penguin, 1965.

Ovidius, Publius Naso. *Fasti.* Translated by Anne Wiseman and Peter Wiseman. New York: Oxford Univ. Press, 2013.

———. *The Metamorphoses of Ovid.* Translated by Mary M. Innes. New York: Penguin Books, 1993.

Plutarch. *Fall of the Roman Republic.* Edited by Seager Robin. Translated by Rex Warner. 1958. Reprint, Harmondsworth, Middlesex, England: Penguin Books, 2005.

———. *Roman Lives: A Selection of Eight Roman Lives.* Translated by Robin Waterfield. Oxford: Oxford University Press, 2008.

Rüpke, Jörg. *The Roman Calendar from Numa to Constantine: Time, History, and the Fasti.* Hoboken, N.J.: John Wiley & Sons, 2011.

Starr, Chester G. *The Ancient Romans.* Oxford: Oxford University Press, 1971.

Suetonius, Gaius Tranquillus. *The Twelve Caesars*. Translated by John Carew Rolfe. Mineola, New York: Dover Publications, Inc, 2018.

Tullius, Marcus Cicero. *The Nature of the Gods*. Translated by P.G. Walsh. Oxford: Oxford University Press, 1998.

Virgilius, Publius Maro. *Aeneid*. Translated by Frederick Ahl. Oxford: Oxford University Press, 2008.

————. *Georgics*. Translated by Peter Fallon. Oxford: Oxford University Press, 2009.

Warrior, Valerie M. *Roman Religion: A Sourcebook*. Newburyport, MA: Focus Pub./R. Pullins Co, 2002.

————. Warrior, Valerie M. *Roman Religion*. Cambridge: Cambridge University Press, 2006.

Ancient Greek Holidays by Mab Borden offers profound insights into the sacred days, months and seasons of ancient Greece. Renowned for meticulous research and vivid descriptions, Borden skillfully details each sacred day, revealing the honored deity and associated social and ritual activities. The book explains the interconnectedness between celestial rhythms and religious observances. Also included are appendices that enhance understanding. Readers journey through festivals dedicated to Gods such as Zeus, Athena and Apollo, gaining insights into the rituals, ceremonies and beliefs shaping ancient Greek spirituality. This book transports readers to a time when daily life was intricately connected to the divine, inspiring reflection on their own spiritual practices and inviting appreciation of the profound beauty of the sacred rhythms that shaped Greek society.

Ancient Egyptian Holidays, part of the Ancient Holidays series by Mab Borden, explores the intricate relationship between religious observances, agricultural practices and the sacred calendar of the Ancient Egyptians. It vividly portrays the cycles of sowing, cultivation and harvesting intertwined with deity worship, from the Festival of the Nile Inundation to the Feast of Opet. This book unveils the profound connection between ancient Egyptians' spiritual beliefs and agricultural livelihood, offering readers a rich mosaic of cultural traditions and rituals marking each month and season. Borden, known for meticulous research and vivid descriptions, skillfully brings these celebrations to life, inviting readers to reflect on their own spiritual connections to nature. It is an essential companion for those seeking a deeper understanding of ancient Egyptian civilization and its wisdom.

Come visit us at the
Witches' Almanac website

www.TheWitchesAlmanac.com

Aradia
Gospel of the Witches
Charles Godfrey Leland

ARADIA IS THE FIRST work in English in which witchcraft is portrayed as an underground old religion, surviving in secret from ancient Pagan times.

- Used as a core text by many modern Neo-Pagans.
- Foundation material containing traditional witchcraft practices
- This special edition features appreciations by such authors as Paul Huson, Raven Grimassi, Judika Illes, Michael Howard, Christopher Penczak, Myth Woodling, Christina Oakley Harrington, Patricia Della-Piana, Jimahl di Fiosa and Donald Weiser. A beautiful and compelling work, this edition is an up to date format, while keeping the text unchanged. 172 pages $16.95

The ABC of Magic Charms
Elizabeth Pepper

Mankind has sought protection from mysterious forces beyond mortal control. Humans have sought the help of animal, mineral, vegetable. The enlarged edition of *Magic Charms from A to Z*, guides us in calling on these forces. $12.95

The Little Book of Magical Creatures
Elizabeth Pepper and Barbara Stacy

AN UPDATE of the classic *Magical Creatures*, featuring Animals Tame, Animals Wild, Animals Fabulous—plus an added section of enchanting animal myths from other times, other places. *A must for all animal lovers.* $12.95

The Witchcraft of Dame Darrel of York
Charles Godfrey Leland, Introduction by Robert Mathiesen

A beautifully reproduced facsimile of the illuminated manuscript shedding light on the basis for a modern practice. A treasured by those practicing Pagans, as well as scholars.   Standard Hardcover $65.00 or Exclusive full leather bound, numbered and slipcased edition $145.00

DAME FORTUNE'S WHEEL TAROT: A PICTORIAL KEY
Paul Huson

Based upon Paul Huson's research in *Mystical Origins of the Tarot, Dame Fortune's Wheel Tarot* illustrates for the first time the earliest, traditional Tarot card interpretations as collected in the 1700s by Jean-Baptiste Alliette. In addition to detailed descriptions, full color reproductions of Huson's original designs for all 79 cards.

WITCHES ALL

A Treasury from past editions, is a collection from *The Witches' Almanac* publications of the past. Arranged by topics, the book, like the popular almanacs, is thought provoking and often spurs the reader on to a tangent leading to even greater discovery. It's perfect for study or casual reading,

GREEK GODS IN LOVE

Barbara Stacy casts a marvelously original eye on the beloved stories of Greek deities, replete with amorous oddities and escapades. We relish these tales in all their splendor and antic humor, and offer an inspired storyteller's fresh version of the old, old mythical magic.

MAGIC CHARMS FROM A TO Z

A treasury of amulets, talismans, fetishes and other lucky objects compiled by the staff of *The Witches' Almanac*. An invaluable guide for all who respond to the call of mystery and enchantment.

LOVE CHARMS

Love has many forms, many aspects. Ceremonies performed in witchcraft celebrate the joy and the blessings of love. Here is a collection of love charms to use now and ever after.

MAGICAL CREATURES

Mystic tradition grants pride of place to many members of the animal kingdom. Some share our life. Others live wild and free. Still others never lived at all, springing instead from the remarkable power of human imagination.

CELTIC TREE MAGIC

Robert Graves in *The White Goddess* writes of the significance of trees in the old Celtic lore. *Celtic Tree Magic* is an investigation of the sacred trees in the remarkable Beth-Luis-Nion alphabet and their role in folklore, poetry and mysticism.

MOON LORE

As both the largest and the brightest object in the night sky, and the only one to appear in phases, the Moon has been a rich source of myth for as long as there have been mythmakers.

MAGIC SPELLS
AND INCANTATIONS

Words have magic power. Their sound, spoken or sung, has ever been a part of mystic ritual. From ancient Egypt to the present, those who practice the art of enchantment have drawn inspiration from a treasury of thoughts and themes passed down through the ages.

LOVE FEASTS

Creating meals to share with the one you love can be a sacred ceremony in itself. With the Witch in mind, culinary adept Christine Fox offers magical menus and recipes for every month in the year.

RANDOM RECOLLECTIONS
III, IV

Pages culled from the original (no longer available) issues of *The Witches' Almanac,* published annually throughout the 1970s, are now available in a series of tasteful booklets. A treasure for those who missed us the first time around, keepsakes for those who remember.